HRD IN GOVERNMENT AND PRIVATE SECTOR

A Comparative Perspective

HRD
IN GOVERNMENT AND PRIVATE SECTOR
A Comparative Perspective

Dr. P. KRISHNA MOORTHY

AKANSHA PUBLISHING HOUSE
NEW DELHI-110002 (INDIA)

AKANSHA PUBLISHING HOUSE
4649-B/21, Ansari Road
Darya Ganj, New Delhi - 110 002
Ph.: 23263193 / 9811582579 / 09435116718
Fax: 011-23263193
Email: ektabooks@yahoo.com

HRD in Government and Private Sector: A Comparative Perspective

First Published 2008

ISBN 978–81–8370–151–8

PRINTED IN INDIA

Published by Akansha Publishing House, New Delhi and Printed at Aryan Enterprises, Delhi.

CONTENTS

FOREWORD

The basic, fundamental and primordial factor for the entire advancement of mankind right from inventing farming system and reaching up to nuclear energy and in between multifarious inventions—technological and industrial, the development factor is what we may call 'The Human Factor'. It is the individual interest and initiative imbued with knowledge and his commitment to excelling in work, working with others in a group situation either as a subordinate or as a super ordinate it is well neigh impossible to imagine the advancement of man, his enormous contribution to progress, development and in a word civilization. The primary principle for any achievement or progress is working together. In all human work situations you always find in all societies and cultures a worker and supervisor. It implies management of activities, co-ordinating the work and accomplishing the said goals.

The concepts of HRD and HRM have gradually gained unquestionable importance in all fields of organised activity. In one sense HRD may be construed as a raw material to be enriched to the anticipated standards the way in which the human enriched raw material – the human factor and in what meaningful, wise and maximal ways it is to be utilized and managed to accomplish the objectives of the organization is the function of Human Resource Management. In one sense HRD and HRM can be compared to scissors. If it were to be operatively sharp and efficient both parts of the scissors the lower and upper should be sharpened. Let us consider the lower part, the employee (HRD) and the upper part, as the Management (HRM). Let us think the employee in the organization is knowledgeable, talented, efficient and committed to task assigned to him but the management or manager does not recognise the efficiency of the employee fails to utilize his services, the objectives of the organization are effected. On the other hand, the management is efficient and the employees are not properly trained and motivated the performance on the part of the workers is very poor. As mentioned above they are to be likened to the two parts of the scissors which are to be equally sharp to perform and reach the objectives.

The present study brings out an interesting contrast in between a Department of Industries in Government and a private manufacturing organization, Amara Raja Batteries. The study analyses in depth the HRD components in both organizations. When we look at the comparative picture here between Government and private concern, we find as outlined in the analysis of the book, the private agency enjoys more of freedom inducting new ideas, principles, recognizing the employee's capabilities and leadership, encouraging effective interpersonal relations and considerable freedom to them in allotting their task.

As a contrast this kind of encouragement, recognition, motivation and work culture are lacking in the Government sector as brought out in the present study in respect to the Department of Industries, Andhra Pradesh.

The importance of HRD and HRM is an ever growing factor and an eye-opener to the management systems all over the world. You may have advanced technology, highly developed machinery and all gadgets in fields of life but the principal factor for success and achievement is the *Human Factor*. In short, it is the employees and the management system that matter ultimately for success of any endeavour. The present book beautifully brings out the essentiality of HRD and HRM and the way in which the two factors are to be meaningfully, wisely and productively utilized. I may point out this brief study is an eye-opener to all those interested in promoting any kind of enterprise with due recognition to the individual employee and equally acknowledging the efficiency of the management system.

- Dr. E.D. Setty

Was Consultant to :

UNESCAP, UNESCO, CEC, AIT, Bangkok, Thailand

LIPI – Indonesia, BRAC – Bangladesh

Dr. MCRHRD Institute of AP

Senior Research Fellow, UNCRD, Japan

Formerly Faculty at Asian Institute of Technology, Bangkok

Professor at Maharshi Institute of Management, Bangalore

PREFACE

The present study brings out an interesting comparative perspective in the realm of HRD between a Department of Industries Government of Andhra Pradesh and a private manufacturing organisation. It highlights some elements of uniformity and spells out significant gaps especially in the role that is played *vis-à-vis* HRD by the Government Department. It clearly brings out the freedom that is exercised by the private organisation in enhancing the role of HRD in accomplishing its major goals. Chapter 2 briefly reviews literature related to HRD. Chapter 3 is detailed discussion and analysis of training as a major contributor to HRD. Chapter 4 in an analytical way highlights relevance of HRM to HRD. Since it is a comparative study chapter 5 spells in detail profiles of organisations selected for the study. Chapter 6 analyses responses secured from the respondents of department of industry and Chapter 7 similarly brings out in an analytical sense the responses from the Private Organisation. Chapter 8 compares and contrasts the responses obtained from both the organisations and finally in a logical sense. Chapter 9 spells out the findings based on the study and provides some suggestions to improve the role that is played by HRD in all organisations.

Dr. P. Krishna Moorthy

ACKNOWLEDGEMENTS

I would like to express my profoundest thanks to Dr. E.D. Setty for his kind foreword to the book. I owe a great deal of thanks and indebtedness to Prof. P. Murali, formerly Vice Chancellor of S.V. University for his encouragement and guidance during my doctoral programme as my advisor. I take this opportunity to express my sincere thanks to the administrative personnel of Department of Industries and the management of Amara Raja Batteries.

I owe a great deal of thanks to my Mother-in-law Smt. E. Vishalakshi and my devoted wife E. Geethanjali for her encouragement and moral support throughout my preparation of material of this publication. I express my deep appreciation and sincere thanks to Mr. A. Mallikarjun who has been supportive through out my work on this manuscript. My special thanks to K. Murali Krishna who has with all sincerity prepared this manuscript for publication.

I should also record here the tender patience and innocent encouragement extended to me by my beloved two sons namely P. Sai Sreenivas Prasad and P. Sai Vamsi.

I express my deep appreciation and thanks to Sri. M.P. Misra of Akansha Publishing House, New Delhi for publishing this book.

Dr. P. KRISHNA MOORTHY

1

INTRODUCTION

"In the ultimate analysis the wealth of a nation is its people".
- Historian Arnold Toynbee

"The Management to make substantial capital investment on human resources to develop human beings in the organization through training organizing and developing the people at work so that they will be able to make the business productive with the help of the best contribution of the people at work".
- Peter F. Drucker, The Father of Management

"The enterprise is the People"

- Konosuke Matsushita

[1]Human Resources Development (HRD) perhaps is one of the most misunderstood concepts. It has lent itself to get limited to corporate sector while the real meaning of HRD extends to all people and is boundary less. HRD is as old as the existence of human beings and perhaps the reason for the very existence of human beings. Without development the human species may have ceased to exist. Contributions to HRD came from all fields and especially from Psychology. Sigmund Freud, Hawthorne studies, the work of BF Skinner which has formed the basis of programmed instruction and

teaching machines (the principles of which are being used extensively by IT sector today), David Mc Lelland, Kurt Lewin and others have all laid solid foundations for most of what is known as and used as HRD in the corporate sector. Indian HRD has its roots in Psychology and Learning. Any one who revisits HRD Department set up in 1975 in Larsen & Toubro will discover "competence building" and "facilitation of learning" as the main underlying themes behind the department itself.

A word about emergence of Human Resource Development

[2]Earlier over 90 percent of the organisations established themselves and evolved their principles of Management without any idea of a series of Management theories profounded by experienced observers with respect to production and productivity within stipulated time. Each organisation on its own experience evolved certain principles with respect to the main functions of Management. We can think of different types of organisations in terms of their ownership, size, their location, the kind of products they manufactured, the kind of people or the mixed ethnic groups employed in the organisations. Depending on these variables the principles in planning the organisational structure and design in terms of centralization, decentralization, delegation of authority and power, the kind of leadership and the measures adopted in controlling and integrating the goals and objectives of the organisation were of varied type. That is, it ranged from highly centralized to marginally decentralized forms, autocratic, task-oriented, to a little employee-oriented.

The principles of Planning, Organising, Leading and Controlling in the organisations reflected of earlier political system, social structure and cultural values with predominantly authoritarian management reinforced by bureaucratic style of functioning. In such a climate, the individual employee was viewed and used as a human raw material, a worker, ignoring his personal feelings, ideas, views and his job-related and life-related needs and his career development. The Management in the past to a large extent, expected the unquestioning behaviour and obedience on the part of the employees and surprisingly, the employees too accepted it as a norm and what was expected of them. But today, the conditions are changed and changing with the gradual increase of education, communication, endowment of rights and privileges to the employees, diffusion and wider spread of knowledge, skills and technology that mattered in a variety of organisations, emergence of trade unions and increased prominence gained by industrial relations, human resources in any organisation became a precious material which is to be respected, nurtured, motivated and promoted for the good and advancement of the individual, his organisation and the larger society.

Home as a Model for Human Resource Development

[3]Here, we may take home and what it constitutes as a model for human resource development. Right from the primitive stage of mankind until today irrespective of the nature and composition of family in any culture, home is considered to be sacrosanct. Home is one where an individual could depend upon and meet his emotional needs. Home could be taken as a synonym of family. When it comes to the family, right across millennia we had different types of families: extended family, joint family, conjugal family and nuclear family. Even sometimes, an entire clan comprising several individuals functions as a family irrespective of the structure, functions and authority that the family enjoyed and yielded in respect of the individual in the family. Home in the sense of family has been the ultimate source of dependency for people. The very word Home speaks of something positive, something tender, something supportive, something

dependable and very close to one's heart. The function of training and management of human and material resource started only with the family. Home is a mental construct. The home headed by the mother and father could be taken as the primary mini-fundamental human organisation. It is impossible to think in terms of any discrimination practiced in the family by the parents or other remembers of the family. The parents of the family always try to nurture and bring up all their children as effective and productive human individuals. When we think of human resource development, here the management of an organisation stands for and constitutes the parents in a family. Without investing on individual employees and developing their knowledge, skills and required attitudinal changes, no organisation can expect a successful move and growth. Here the idea is let the management function as parents of the family bestowing attention on each individual employees, as if he is the child in a family and think in terms of his growth and development and make use of him towards realizing the vision, goals and objectives of the organisation.

The home has the concern for all its members. As in the case of the family, for some of the new entrants in an organisation, it is a formative period for them as in the case of infants and teens in the family. The family develops a sense of identity and belongingness among the members of the family. Home is not physical but it is a mental, sentimental, emotional, abstract picture. Whatever may be the contacts and changes that take place in the life of the individual and whatever may be physical distance between the home and the individual, home remains as a psychological anchor and bedrock. The predominant factor in the home is the love, affection and concern for each other. And one expects the same kind of love and concern for the employees in an organisation shown by the management.

Family as mentioned above is the basic, primary institution of human society despite changes in the structure and functions of the family. The ultimate aim of an individual or a collectivity is towards growth, development and happiness of the individual. The idea of taking home as a model for human resource development depends on what the home constitutes, what it stands for and how it functions, what a noble concept the home is, and can all the organisations which are secondary groups become homes in respect of recognizing, carrying and developing the individual employees in the organisation. Of course, it stands primarily for the advantage of the organisation and secondarily towards the growth of the individual personnel.

Role of a Mother as a model to any Organisation:

Whether it is a government department, a public enterprise or a private organization, it is needless to stress that people are the organization and they could be compared to numeral one and rest of things could be zeros or any numbers. If we place zeros after one, it carries weight, if it were to be placing one after zero it means nothing. There is a great need for any organization to play the role of a MOTHER and see how a mother prepares, fosters, nurtures, educates, and trains her children. The MOTHER is to be a model to any organization. The mother role is to be adopted by all organizations vis-à-vis the employees and create a sense of belonging and a sense of pride among the employees, that they identify themselves with the organization in-Toto. This could be achieved not only through incentives and training and career planning and development but to a great extent it depends on the attitude on the part of the management towards the employees and the way in which they are communicated with and treated. Every employee irrespective of his role and status in the organization is to be treated as an important contributing human component for the activity and success of the organization.

The *simplest definition* of Human Resources Development is organized learning experience provided by employers within a specified period of time to bring about the possibilities of performance improvement and on personal growth. The number of activity areas in HRD are the following:

1. Training - Learning focused on the present job of the learner.
2. Education - Learning focused on a future job of the learner.
3. Development - Not job focused.

HRD reflects a new philosophy, a new outlook, approach, and strategy, which views an organization's manpower as its resources and assets, and not as liabilities or mere hands.

Resources are the means which can be drawn on. They are collective means for production, support and defense, as well as a source of strength and aid. Human resources are human wealth or means that can be drawn on. Human capital or manpower resources of an organization can be treated as its human resources. It can otherwise be understood as the resourcefulness of the human beings or people available for an organization.

Based on the above activities we can understand that the Human Resource Development (HRD)[4] Department has the following functions.

- ❖ Discovers knowledge and skills relevant HRD, pertaining to its philosophy, processes and implementation through experiments.
- ❖ Builds a storehouse of knowledge and skills in HRD with professional approach and disseminates HRD knowledge and skills.

- ❖ Acting as a clearing for all HRD related activities, evaluating the impact of HRD processes and feedback for improvement of results.
- ❖ Maintaining an efficient information system.

Importance of Resources (Natural and Human)

It is interesting to note that natural resources that a country is endowed with does not automatically make it rich. But it is the human resources that harness and wisely utilize the natural resources towards material affluence and richness of life. The following examples show the paradox in respect of natural and human resources where in it is the human resources that account for the rich or poor state of a country.

RESOURCE RICH	:	RICH USA, CANADA, BRAZIL
RESOURCE RICH	:	POOR MANY OF THE AFRICAN AND LATIN AMERICAN COUNTRIES AND IN A SENSE INDIA TOO.
RESOURCE POOR	:	RICH JAPAN, ISRAEL
RESOURCE POOR	:	POOR NEPAL, BANGLADESH

The same paradox applies to some of the states in India.

In generic terms, human resources can be defined as the total knowledge, skills, creative abilities, talents and aptitudes of an organization's workforce, as well as the values, attitudes, approaches and beliefs of the individuals involved in the affairs of the organization. It is the sum total or aggregate of inherent abilities, acquired knowledge and skills represented by the talents and aptitudes of the employed persons in an organization.

Human resources approach takes into consideration the potentiality and vitality of the people available for the organization. Even in an age of automation as of today, manpower is the most essential and indispensable resource of any organization. Resourcefulness of various categories of people say: managers, scientists and research people, executives, supervisors, workers (skilled, unskilled) and all such people available for the organization to be drawn on, can be treated as human resources. In fact, without appropriate human resources, no business or organization can exist and grow. This is, perhaps, the reason why human resources management has become the focus of attention of progressive organizations of today.

Human resources management is the process of managing the people of an organization with a humane approach. Human resources approach to manpower enables the manager to view his people as an important, if not the most important resource. It is a benevolent approach to develop and effectively utilize the manpower not only for the benefit of the organization but for the growth, development and self satisfaction of the concerned people. Thus, human resources management is a system that focuses on human resources development, on the one hand, and effective management of people on the other.

As a result of the fundamental changes in attitudes, approaches, outlook, philosophy, perspective and practices emerged in the personnel area in the form of human resources management (HRM) strategy, it has become necessary for every organization to develop skills, talents, potentialities, capabilities and attitudes of company's own people to meet the emerging challenges. Hence, HRD (human resources development) policies have been adopted by many organizations. It is now-a-days spreading to many others. HRD strategies are supposed to bring forth necessary changes in skills, capabilities and attitudes of people who are required to cope with the emerging changes. Thus, HRD has become an integral part of human resources management.

The new HRD approach, that stresses the need for developing the organization's own people to suit the updated technology, modernization of machinery and equipments and the changing trends in attitudes and approaches, necessitates to develop individual employee in accordance with his aspirations and potentialities on the one hand, and the organization's requirement on the other. This is what the HRD does. Quite often, Organization Development (OD) programmes are effectively integrated with the HRD programmes. Of course, OD programmes are the programmes which the OD interventionists prescribe for the effectiveness of the organization. It need not be what the individual members of the organization seek. HRD interventionists primarily seek to know what the individuals seek to have, and then try to match it with the organizational needs. Training and development programmes form part of OD, while training and development are the most decisive aspects of HRD too.

Firstly, development of leadership (developing leaders capable of working in multicultural environments both within their organizations and across national boundaries). Challenges facing management of people are monumental in the contemporary business and development world. Factors like changes in the world economic and political system, technological aspects and human values, tension over protecting jobs with national boundaries versus looking offshore for cheaper labour costs so as to remain world competitive, fresh economic policy issues stemming from the transformation of economies and job structures, increase of high technology jobs, all such factors necessitate to develop leadership vital for effective actuation.

Secondly, development of a new organizational culture. A revolutionary cultural change triggered by globalization of business and the resultant demand for strong operational managers necessitate a greater reinforcement in the human resources system. Human resources development to cope with the corporate cultural change is the need of the hour. "It is important to make the implicit explicit: to continually examine the culture through a variety of feedback mechanisms, mapping out the culture, assessing where the organization is, where it wants to go, carefully identifying strategies for change which constantly deal with the cultural gaps, and working the organization culture in relationship to the particular national culture in which it is embedded".

Thirdly, human resources development must focus on new organizational forms. Human resource planning and development strategy must be rightly coupled with business strategies to the extent that the whole organization may take the shape of a viable global organization. New concepts regarding what is work and how to redistribute tasks, redefine roles, authority relationships, and sources of power must be based on the new models emerging globally. Recruiting, selecting, developing, rotating, and managing human resources must aid such a global organization with a new form and perspective.

Human resource development must be able to develop overall capability of individual employees of an organization, and discover and exploit their own potentials for the common goals of the organizations to which they belong, for the betterment of themselves and their families, and for the country as a whole. For this purpose appropriate job design and succession plan must be integrated with any human resource development programme. In fact, HRD approach may take into account the principle of *"form-storm-norm-perform"*.

Six dimensions of human resource development, may be mentioned here. These six dimensions are: (a). Performance appraisal; (b) Potential appraisal; (c) Employee counseling; (d) Career development and planning; (e) Training; and (f) Organizational Development. In general any human resource development programme must enable the organization's people to acquire and sharpen their capabilities to perform well on their respective jobs, develop and stimulate their potentialities, and to help them make their best contribution to develop an organization culture of team spirit, cordial relationship, human values and oneness of the management and its people. From this view point, HRD enables an executive to gain a job that provides variety and challenge to one's ability and competence, opportunity to learn and develop skills and competence, social support and recognition at work place, opportunity to relate what an individual performs and produce to his social life, and feeling that work would lead to a desirable future.

Thus, HRD is a continuous process, which matches organizational needs for human resources and the individual needs for a career development. It enables the individuals to gain their best human potential by attaining a total all-round development. It promotes dignity of employment of every employee of an organization, and provides opportunities for team work, personal development and career development. Hence a well-planned HRD system must be a part of human resource management of every organization. Such a human resource development system may have the following elements:

(i) Development of leadership and organizational commitment;
(ii) Career planning and development;
(iii) Performance Appraisal;
(iv) An adequate reward system;
(v) Potential Appraisal;
(vi) Effective counseling;
(vii) Well formulated Human Resource Information System (HRIS);

(viii) An effective grievance handling;
(ix) Management development;
(x) Technical development;
(xi) Supervisory development;
(xii) Organization development;
(xiii) Training and educating;
(xiv) Succession planning;
(xv) Employee welfare; and
(xvi) Feedback.

These elements are presented in the following diagram

[5]Diagram. A Model for Human Resource Development

Diagram

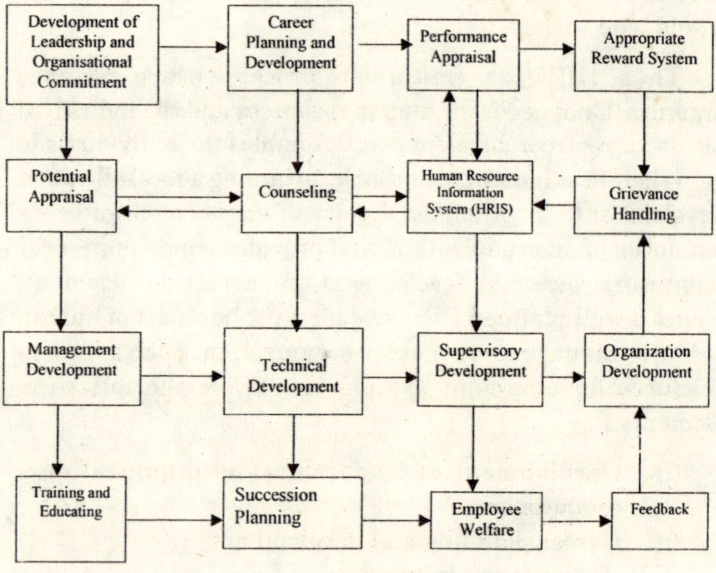

5. ***Source:-*** *Human Resources Management and Human Relations by V.P. Michael, Himalaya Publishing House, 1997, pg.156.*

Every organization needs to develop leadership and sincere organizational commitment of its people. Hence, it is proper if the HRD starts with developing leadership and people with organizational commitment. As the organization needs its people to have sincere organizational commitment, every employee has his or her own aspirations to have a good career. Hence, career planning and development for every employee in the organization should go hand in hand with leadership development.

Career planning and development must be followed by performance appraisal and reward system which should motivate the employees to make their best contribution to the organizational goals and objectives. Leadership development must also be followed by potential appraisal which enable the HRM to determine the potentiality of every individual employee to hold critical positions and tackle critical situations. Counseling, which includes career counseling, motivation counseling and problem solving counseling, facilitates career planning and development, while a human resources information system must function at the center of HRD system. Effective and timely grievance handling must be a part of every HRD system, since no effort for human resource development can bear real fruit without timely grievance handling.

Developing managers to handle organizational resources including human resources and activities effectively is the need of every organization, particularly in the context of rapidly changing business environment. It must be followed by technological and technical development. Updating the organization's technology, modernization of the plant, and automation need appropriate people for which human development programmes are required. The actual operation takes place at the supervisory level, and hence supervisory development is the crux of HRD. Developing the workforce development is included in the supervisory development function. All such development programmes must result in organization development. Obviously OD becomes a part of HRD.

Training and educating makes an important method of human development in an organization, which enables an organization to prepare its people for various positions. Hence, succession planning goes with human development, employee welfare has a long way to go in motivating the people of every organization making the HRD intervention effective. Hence, employee welfare is integrated with the HRD model presented here. Feedback also makes a part of this model just like any other management model. Effective feedback goes with every developed organization. Proper grievance handling is, at the same time necessary for the feedback system to function effectively. Some of the steps of HRD model are examined below separately.

Managers, over the years, have relied on training the people as a part of developing their organizations. In recent times Management By Objective, Managerial Grid, Transaction Analysis, Quality Circles And Quality of Work Life programmes have found favour with many organizations. Both professional and traditional managers now harp on fads of one of these names profusely for portraying the progressive nature of their organizations. For an effective human resource development, there must be a constant effort on the part of management to develop their people. The use of these methods and techniques is also not ruled out.

Training is an instrument of developing the employees or workforce by enriching the skills and improving the human behaviour, which result in organization development adequate for the accomplishment of objectives from time to time. It helps organizations and individuals to develop themselves in consonance with the changing needs of the environment in which they survive, operate and progress. Training in technology, profession, organizational behaviour, and management development are common. Both on-the-job and off-the-job training are important.

In systematically operating a training system in an organization, the human resource manager may formulate a systematic pattern. It may include: (1) Assessment of training needs; (2) Determination of gaps; (3) Designing training programmes; (4) Identifying resource persons; (5) Preparation of training budgets; (6) Preparation of training materials; (7) Organization of training programmes; (8) Evaluation of training effectiveness; and (9) Revising training pattern or training modules wherever necessary.

Manpower is indisputably the basic resource. It is the indispensable means of converting other resources for the use and benefit of mankind. In the words of the late President Kennedy of USA. "It is not mere possession of natural resources that makes a nation strong and viable, it is fundamentally the employment of these resources that is significant". One could see the gradual emergence, slow realization and recognition and the importance of the human factor for development and success in all walks of life. This recognition of HRD was first realized in the industrial and service domains all over the world. The employees in any organisation at any point of time are not totally enlightened, motivated committed in accomplishing the tasks assigned to them and effectively working in groups with mutual trust and support. Any industry may have sophisticated machinery, requisite infrastructure, detailed plans for production but the critical contributing factor is the man behind the machine. Taking man as a pivotal factor attention is paid in providing knowledge, skills and requisite attitudinal changes. Conducive to effective performance of their tasks and thus contributing to higher productivity and generating a conducive organisational culture where every employee feels at home, committed to his work. The importance as mentioned above for HRD grew in different parts of the world in a sporadic way. Managements have learnt the importance of HRD through the process of trial and error in general.

To begin with managements were interested mainly making profits and the importance accorded to the employees was rather of a differential nature without bestowing attention to the human side of employees' contribution. In other words the management more often expected the employees to perform their best without looking into that would facilitate and empower the best contribution from the employees. Since the employees were in most cases in dire need of jobs to begin with what they had to endure ill treatment and bad working conditions. Over a period of time, the employees also were awakened, gained strength and began questioning, directly and indirectly drawing the attention of management in enriching their knowledge and skills so that their contribution for the industrial service will be maximum. There is another factor which also contributed to the importance of HRD in organisations. Here, we may mention unionism as a movement all over the world which drew the attention of different management systems. Here, we see the predominant interest of management as business endeavour and need for producing quality goods and rendering quality services and gradual increase of awareness.

When we speak of enriching knowledge and skills and developing right attitude on the part of the employees preparing them and motivating them to strive for their career advancement and simultaneously contribute to the progress of the organization where they employed. In this context we emphasize as we mentioned the inputs that are briefly explained below.

1.	Knowledge	:	Related to expected function (role of the individual employee) at present and future
2.	Skill	:	Once learnt and developed remains constant, but as the nature of work changes with the introduction of new technology and competitiveness certain skills are to be upgraded and new skills are to be learnt and practices to meet the demands and challenges in the work situation.
3.	Attitude		On the part of the employee in terms of interest, commitment, determination working towards standard of excellence.

For any effective performance, establishing a standard of excellence, three components of action are essential. They are: knowledge, skills and positive attitude. If any one of these is low, missing or unutilized or under utilized resultant thing would be poor performance, low quality of product. Usually only two components knowledge and skills are considered required for any job, but often we do not take into consideration, the individual employees' attitude (disposition) towards his work as well as towards his organisation. [6] In recruitment of personnel and enhancing HRD in any organisation one may have to prepare and develop positive, job related functions and attitude on the part of the employee. When we speak of the attitude which is so subtle which can be observed only through action and individuals behaviour this attitude of the employee has several dimensions –image of himself, his disposition towards colleagues, superiors and the organisaticn where he works. Often in personal guidance, mostly focus is more on knowledge and relatively less on skills and takes attitudinal disposition for granted or not given much importance. Unless some friction takes place something wrong committed by the employee and sometimes-unfriendly interaction with the colleagues, then only we realize and try to find out the reasons for this kind of behaviour and positive changes in him through guidance, counselling and training putting him in a group situation.

The management once it realizes the need for enriching the knowledge, upgrading the skills, bringing in positive attitude on the part of the employee, it not only benefits the organization and simultaneously it enriches the employee and brings in him a quality of change. [7]Often people think that the training imparted to the employees is for the benefit of organization, though it is true and on the other hand the organization is getting benefited it is the employee who is equally or more than equally benefited through on – the- job training. Here one may think of input and out- put and a combination of inputs and outputs and their result of contribution. We may think of certain essential abilities or dispositions for the successful result. Often if one element is missing in the combination of input the result will be quiet different. There may be two positive things and one missing thing, the output will not be at expected standard. Here we may briefly look into the inputs and results thereof.

Sl. No	*Inputs*		*Results (Output)*
1.	Adequate knowledge – Poor operational skills – poor attitude.	:	Performance is very poor
2.	Inadequate knowledge – rich operational skills – poor attitude	:	Performance is poor
3.	Inadequate knowledge – Inadequate Skills, positive attitude	:	Comparatively better performance
4.	Adequate knowledge, requisite skills & positive attitude	:	Expected and anticipated performance

Source: Researcher's own observation.

The above combinations are found in most of the employees. The idea here is if any one of the 3 components is in sufficient the performance will be poor. And also the individual level of work satisfaction will be poor when he discovers what is missing in him on the part of employee as well as dissatisfaction on the part of the Management. When we go in for systematic training of the employees (before and after training) the management has to ensure that there is balanced composition of the 3 factors. The 3 components are not static – Knowledge can be improved, skills can be changed. But attitudinal change is rather a difficult process; slowly it can also be changed.

REFERENCES

1. Adopted from "Perspectives on HRD" (Foreword) – Mr. Udai Pareek, Chairman, Academy of HRD & Mr. T V Rao, Chairman, Academic Council, AHRD. Edited by Prof. E.G. Parameswaran.
2. P. Krishna Moorthy, "Dynamics of Change in the Organizational Development" published in Indian Journal of Training & Development (IJTD), October, 2002, New Delhi, India. pp. 72 – 79.
3. Dr. E.D. Setty, Home As a Model for HRD, *Perspectives on HRD,* compiled and Edited by Prof. E.G. Parameswaran, Neel Kamal Publications, Hyderabad, 2002, pp.38-51.
4. T.V. Rao *'HRD & Organisational Effectiveness',* selected readings in HRD by K.Singh, T.V. Rao, B.Nair, Tata Mcgraw Hill Publishing CO. Ltd; 1996, pg-24.
5. Prof. V.P. Michael, *Human Resources Management & Human Relations,* Himalaya Publishing House, Bombay, 1997.pg. 156.
6. Randy L. Desimone, John M. Werner, David M. Harris *"Human Resource Development"* printed and bound Eastern Press, Bangalore Pvt. Ltd. 2005; P.P.1– 26.
7. *Training Reading material on "Human Resource Development"; pp. 18 – 29, given by Dr. MCR HRD IAP.*

2

REVIEW OF LITERATURE

The importance attached to HRD and the way in which it is translated and applied to day – to – day activity pertaining to production of goods, services and administration of overall operation. It is easy theories and speculates the place and importance of HRD in any kind of organization. One may list out the ideal steps to promote HRD and also specify the way in which human resources are to be harnessed, encouraged and sustained for better performance towards increased performance and effective delivery of services.

May be one could see for the past several decades academic efforts have been sincerely utilized to understand the importance of HRD as ever growing, expanding and finally stabilizing itself and significantly contributing to the growth and development of the organization as well as employees engaged in it.

In the following we will briefly look into a few attempts that have been made on significance and importance attached to HRD and the way in which the elements and principles of HRD translate into action in the day to day working of the organization plus providing training to the employees at all levels in the relevant fields so that they become effective instruments in achieving the targets of the organization and meeting its goals.

As mentioned above we may briefly look into a few studies that were carried out earlier which are in way related to HRD.

In business organizations at the early stage the emphasis has been on the management of the employees and not in terms of their knowledge, skills, competence and commitment in respect to the task assigned to them. It was mostly the review or assessment tuned to management and not looking into the requisite knowledge, skill and competence on the part of the Employees. In the beginning the employees in respect to the analysis and evaluation and their competence were not taken seriously into account. Later the organizations realised the need for training the employees in respect to their knowledge, skills, attitude, and aptitude. In this scenario the researcher looks briefly into the literature related to HRD.

The researcher put every effort to look for research based published studies and he could come across the following few studies.

Further it may be pointed out so far as the researcher could look for there have been very few research undertakings in the field of Human Resource Development (HRD). But one comes across several brief articles on several dimensions of HRD. On scanning over long time the researcher could identify and select a few research publications related to the domain of HRD.

It may be pointed here though there is an academic and research need to review studies related to Human Resource Development, it is quite pertinent to have a few reviews here related to Human Resource Management also which is something like a twin brother to HRD.

[1]It is observed that Hawthorne studies, which was carried out in the early 1920's under the leadership of Elton Mayo at the Hawthorne works of the Western Electric Company in the U.S.A., pointed out that (1) the needs for recognition,

security and sense of belonging exert greater impact on workers' productivity than the physical working conditions. A manager can get good output in poor working conditions if the human relationships are good, but he cannot get good output in good working conditions if the human relations are bad; (2) informal groups operating within the organisation exert strong social controls over the work habits and performance of the individual workers; and (3) supervision has a great impact on the bahaviour of the work groups in determining as to whether they will react positively or negatively while working towards the organizational objectives. .

[2]Frederick Harbison and Charles A.Myers (1964) viewed that the concept of human resources has many different meaning, both manpower and human resources refer to and mean people. Human resources could be equated in the "Labour" in the scene of a factory of production, or simply population. Human Resources may also be viewed as a kind of natural resource or a people resource just as we have mineral and forest resources.

[3]Allen, A. Zall (1966) has emphasised that on concern in manpower planning and development of human resources is mainly due to socialisation of the individual to work in organisation as well as an individual. Socialisation involves change in the persons; therefore, when we consider some of the techniques for developing human resources, we should be clear about the changes we have in mind. He further mentions "We are specifically concerned with five kinds of changes, viz., changes in skills, changes in knowledge, changes in attitudes, changes in awareness of self, changes in motivation are the important aspects to promote human resource development. The techniques used for development should be compatible with the type of change that is desired.

[4]As Fowler (1987) has written, the HRM message to top management tends to be very simple. Don't bother too much

about the content or techniques of personnel management, it says. Just manage the context. Get out from behind your desk, bypass the hierarchy, and go and talk to people. That way you will unlock an enormous potential for improved performance.

[5] It has been observed, by Daver R.S., in the Scenario of HRD that the Human Resource Development has played an important role in the development of the human and organisation in future HR will not be accomplished within the HR function; it will also be accomplished by its operating strategies with line managers, other staff managers and strategic partnerships with outside vendors.

[6] It has been observed by Prahalad C.K. & Hamel G, "HRD Challenges in 21st Century" that the world is moving at an extremely fast pace and that the rate of change is continuing to accelerate. It can now be said that we have moved to the era if not just change but an accelerated rate of change. This demands that corrective steps too need to be taken fast. As compared to the past, the twenty-first century corporations are getting to be globally market driven ones with 'invest any-where and share everywhere' concept. The impact of e-commerce with rapidly changing information technology will similarly transform conventional business structures dramatically. These will demand a totally different type of HR strategy and intervention. Following are the four stages of growth and evolution process of the human resources management function.

The four functions are:

1. The Reactive function:
2. The Independent HRD function:
3. The Supportive HRD function:
4. The Integrative HRD function:

[7]Attaining and sustaining competitiveness is essential to service in the context of changes at national and global levels. In such a situation the HRM function has an integrative role to knot the people and their tasks/roles together in harmony. The purpose and focus of HRM function should be to build stronger organizations dedicated to the realization of corporate vision and mission with full commitment to the growing aspirations of its constituents in an environment that demands high productivity, satisfying performance and social responsiveness and responsibility. HRM being a service function, its role should be built taking into consideration the expectations of its client group. Genuine and systematic efforts to make meaningful analysis of expectations should be based principally, on the answer to the following three questions.

1. Who are the customers of the human resource department?
2. What do customers expect from HRM function?
3. What could the HRM department be doing for the customers that it is not doing now?

[8]It has been noted, by William P.A, that a major paradigm shift has taken place with the evolution of the concept of Human Resources Development. The growing recognition of HRD in the management area has brought a revolutionary change in the total scenario of performance appraisal. It has been reflected in terms of use of word to indicate Performance Appraisal and the purpose of Performance Appraisal and corrective measures used.

[9]John Purcell (1993) thinks that 'the adoption of HRM is both a product of and a cause of a significant concentration of power in the hands of management', while the widespread use 'of the language of HRM, if not its practice, is a combination of its intuitive appeal to angers and, more

importantly, a response to the turbulence of product and financial markets'. He asserts that HRM is about the rediscovery of management prerogative.

He considers that HRM policies and practices. when applied within a firm as a break from the past, are often associated with words such as commitment, competence, empowerment, flexibility, culture, performance, assessment, reward, teamwork, involvement, cooperation, harmonization, quality and learning. But 'the danger of descriptions of HRM as modern best-management practice is that they sterotype the past and idealize the future'

[10]It has been pointed out, by Chakraborthy S.K., here in respect to orientation in the context of HRD that all the employees recruited are put through a well structured orientation programme to help them understand what the organisation stands for in terms of its basic philosophy and culture, their role and what is expected of them as also what they can expect from the company. At the orientation training, specific inputs on correct behaviour and courtesies required at the work place are imparted to help the participants make a smooth transition from the institute to the company. At every orientation programme, the trainees are asked to group themselves and understand their life style as it was at the institute. They are asked to visualize life in organisation. The HRD specialist along with the senior member of the organisation then help to understand various processes that go on in the company and the expectations of the organisation of the trainee.

[11]A study was conducted by Rao Mohan, 1996 in a large private hospital in Hyderabad. 50 supervisors from different departments of the hospital were selected as sample. The focus of the study was on HRD Climate, Superior – Subordinate Relationship, personnel policies, Team Spirit, Training, Employee initiative and Management encouragement.

The findings of this study are showed that the climate for HRD at the HRM Department (89.4%); the dental department (69%) the general department (65%) and the lab (60%) was highly favourable, compared to marketing department (14.1%) and accounts department (39%). The low relationship in between superiors and subordinates was due to the constant supervision and control by the top management, stress involved in meeting the targets and inhibitions and lack of confidence in taking initiatives. All the 7 dimensions, having an overall mean score of 3.46 contributed effectively to the HRD climate in the hospital.

[12]It was an article published namely HRD for results: The Agenda by A.B. Siva Kumar

The author pointed out as it is quiet well known that the HRD is a means to an end, and not an end in itself. This end is nothing but a maximum satisfaction of one's higher order needs of recognition, achievement and self-actualization. Further, the author observed Indian organisations that have extended the HRD concept to the shop floor have done extremely well in terms of research. The emphasis has been on empowering the workers to take decisions that concern their immediate work environment. Further, the author observed that whatever HRD philosophy an organisation might have, HRD itself becomes meaningful only if there are certain bottom line results to show and HRD embraces and becomes part of organisational initiatives like Total Quality Management (TQM), which have become the order of the day.

[13]According to Ulrich (1997) there are three explicit relationships between HR practices and the three locales of value, as follows:

- Employees : Morale, commitment, competence and retention

- Customers : Retention, Satisfaction and commitment
- Investors : Profitability, Cost, Growth, Cash flow and margin

Simple logic suggests that HR practices affect each of these practices directly as illustrated below.

HR practices →	Employees :	How does HR affect morale, commitment, competence and retention
HR practices →	Customers :	Retention, Satisfaction and commitment
HR practices →	Investors :	Profitability, Cost, Growth, Cash flow and margin

[14]HRM is something that managements tend to believe in and it could therefore be regarded as simply a notion of how people can best be managed in the interests of the organisation. If this is the case, then concepts such as strategic integration, culture management, commitment and total quality management, and a unitary philosophy (the interests of management and employees coincide) fit in well with the HRM model. Certainly, these notions have entered into the vocabulary of managers and support the idea which something could be broadly described as 'strategic HRM' (although they may not use this phrase) will help them to improve organizational performance in the longer term, although their expectations of what HRM can achieve by the use of various simplistic mechanisms, such as performance related pay, may be unrealistic, as Mabey *et al* (1998) and Gratton *et al* (1999) have demonstrated.

[15]Bhatia S.K. pointed out that increasing evidence of the cost minimisation, low-skill, low pay, corner cutting approach etc and there is much low morale of the evidence of employment practices among small and medium sized

employing organisation indicating a situation more akin to Bleak house than HRD.

[16]Hare, Rama, Dharma or HRD is the driving force of any organisation. Rama invokes your own radiance and Dharma is the duty of the organisation to see that each individual performs to the best of his / her obligations. This Dharma if followed by each organisation, will drive us from an asset based economy to a talent based economy. There is an old saying "Yatha raja Thatha Praja". Under the new definition of HRD it should be "Yatha Praja Thatha Raja" – which means it is the people in the organisation who will determine the leadership.

Globally, it is being recognised today that the Sum total of developments achieved by organisations is in fact, a sum total of individual development.

[17] Professor, E.G. Parameswaran, points out in his article Assumptions, Strategies and Outcomes that the HRD movement is perfectly relevant but it cannot be restricted to the organisational concept. The individuals demand is important, organisational performance is important and human development at the higher societal level is also important. HRD professional should keep this in mind and get out of the narrow constraints of the limited organisational mindset, which they have searched for themselves.

[18] Professor, Udai Pareek an eminent person, while speaking of key functions of HRD says the mission of HRD is to optimise organisational effectiveness through fulfillment and effectiveness of its people. This mission should guide the development of key functions of HRD as mentioned below:

a. Strategic partnering

b. Professionalising HRD

c. Championing for the people

d. Humanising the organisation

e. Organisational self-renewal.

He further states the responsibility of producing persons with such competencies would require re-orientation of some management courses and programmes of development of HRD skills.

[19] While commenting on 'HRD Climate in organisations' the authors T.V. Rao & E. Abraham S.J. based on their wide research and experience in the field expressed that the organisations become dynamic and growth oriented if their people are dynamic and pro-active. Every organisation can do a lot to make their people become dynamic and pro-active through proper selection of such people and nurturing their dynamism and other competencies. Organisations cannot survive beyond a point unless they are continuously prepare their employees to meet the challenges and have an impact on the changing environment. They also come out with an optimal level of development climate essential for facilitating HRD characterized by the following tendencies on the part of the organisation.

- A tendency at all levels starting from top management to the lowest level to treat the people as the most important resource.
- A perception that developing the competencies in the employees is the job of every manager/supervisor.
- Faith in the capability of employees to change and acquire new competencies at any stage of life.
- A tendency to be open in communications and discussion rather than being secretive (fairly free expression of feelings).
- Encouraging risk-taking and experimentation.

- Making efforts to help employees recognize their strengths and weaknesses through feedback.
- A general climate of trust.
- A tendency on the part of employees to be generally helpful to each other and collaborate with each other.
- Team spirit.
- Tendency to discourage stereotypes and favouritism.
- Supportive personnel policies.
- Supportive HRD practices including performance appraisal, training, reward management, potential development, job-rotation and career planning.

The above observations by the authors, is based on results of a questionnaire administered to 1,614 respondents from 41 different organisations. These 41 organisations include different units of large organisations having fairly high decentralized set up.

The entire survey was planned with a view to collect a data and provide feedback to the organisations about their HRD Climate.

[20]The authors T.V. Rao & E. Abraham S.J. have launched their research in Human Resource Development: present trends and future directions and based on their research they have come out with the following suggestions and recommendations:

1) Acquire or sharpen capabilities required to perform various functions associated with their present or expected future roles;

2) Develop their general capabilities as individuals and discover and exploit their own inner potentials for their own and/or organisational development purposes; and

3) Develop an organisational culture in which supervisor-subordinate relationships, teamwork and collaboration among sub-units are strong and contribute to the professional well-being, motivation and pride of employees.

HRD aims at helping people to acquire competencies. The process of acquisition can be facilitated by HRD mechanisms (instruments or subsystems) like performance appraisal, training, OD, feedback and counselling, career development, potential development, job-rotation and rewards.

More recently, in the Handbook of Human Resources Development, 1984, Nadler presents a somewhat reworked definitions. "Human Resources Development is defined as organized learning experiences in a definite time period to increase the possibility of improving job performance (and) growth".

To further delineate his definition of HRD, Nadler offers the following explanations:

1. Organised Learning Experiences:
2. A Definite Time Period:
3. To increase the Possibility:
4. Improving the Job Performance:
5. Growth:

[21]In an interesting analysis of experience from 14 organisations in respect of strategies for developing Human Resources, by T.V. Rao and E. Abraham S.J, the criteria for including 14 organisations as mentioned below are:

1. Recognition of the importance of HRD by these organisations as indicated by:

    a) the establishment of a HRD department; or

b) creation of a new role for managing the HRD function, or

c) investments made for initiating unconventional HRD mechanisms (any mechanism other than training), or

d) adoption of an integrated HRD system.

2. Availability of published literature and/or involvement of the author as an HRD consultant.

The analysis related to the above topic were carried out in the following 14 organisations which is an extensive dealing with HRD as it is practiced in these organisations. Those organisations are listed below:

1. Larsen and Toubro Ltd. (L&T)
2. Crompton Greaves Ltd. (CGL)
3. L&T Construction Group (ECC)
4. Jyothi Ltd.
5. TVS Iyenger & Sons
6. Voltas Ltd.
7. Sundram Fasteners Ltd. (SFL)
8. Bharat Earth Movers Limited (BEML)
9. OD in BHEL, Bhopal
10. Bank of Baroda (BOB)
11. State Bank of India (SBI)
12. Indian Oil Corporation (IOC)
13. Steel Authority of India Limited (SAIL)
14. State Bank of Patiala (SBP)

[22]In a very broad sense (Macro Level) when we look at the Government organisations and private organisations or

enterprises it may be observed that the private organisations relatively are more concerned and pay genuine attention in employing several effective means and methods in the Human Resource Development of their employees since the private organizations are mostly profit oriented and always stand in a competitive environment. But on the other hand, though HRD is given importance in Government Departments both the Central and the State Level comparatively the emphasis is less serious with that of private organisations. Here are the research findings related to the civil servants (I.A.S. Officers) by Mehta:

1. A majority of them felt that people's participation in development is important in development programmes but staff participation in the management of government is not likely to be of any use and in fact, it may worsen the situation.

2. About 86 percent of the top managers interviewed also felt that the government employees lacked competence for handling the increasingly complex jobs in the government.

3. About 76 percent of the top level IAS officers could not recall any instances of their efforts to develop their own staff to grow and develop.

These findings demonstrate very clearly the need for developing HRD orientation in IAS officers.

It is a myth to say that IAS officers (who are largely responsible for managing various complicated affairs of the country) do not have resources to develop their own staff who can in turn help them to accomplish their objectives better. An officer who offers the explanation that he cannot do it without somebody else's permission is only covering his own lack of initiative and reluctance to change in the name of his boss or politician. If IAS officers cannot bring about these changes no one else can, and to practice most of what has been stated in this chapter one's own conviction is more essential than someone else's permission.

[23]A study was conducted on HRD Climate in a Co-operative Department from different localities namely Gandhi Nagar, Ahmedabad, Rajkot, Baroda and Surat. Sample Size is 117 employees from all the above localities were taken from the co-operative department and a questionnaire was administered. Focus of the study is on (a) Work culture, (b) Work behaviour, (c) Morale, (d) Commitment and (e) Motivation.

The findings of the study are singles out Human Resource Development is the base of all developments. Other resources like physical and financial resources only be activated through the agency and Human Resources.

[24]A study was conducted, by Anil Kumar Singh, on HRD practices and philosophy of management in Indian organisations (public & private organisations). The sample for the study consisted of 95 respondents from two private sector organisations and 119 respondents from two public sector organisations.

The objectives of this study are to:

- Examine the assumptions of the top management about the people working in the organisation.
- Understand the social organisation through HRD belief and the philosophy of management in the organisation.
- Examine the nature of differences in the philosophy of management subscribed to by the organisation towards employees working in the public and the private sector.
- Examine the nature of relationship between HRD practices represented by planning, recruitment,

selection, performance evaluation, training and development, career management and rewards and the philosophy of management in the private and the public sector organisation.

The focus of the study is on planning, recruitment, selection, performance evaluation, T & D, career management and rewards.

The results of the study are paradoxical on one hand while Managers believed in shared objectives, participation and individual control yet they tend to have serious doubts about the capacity to demonstrate initiative, individual action and leadership.

The top Managers of the Public Sector and their public documents show belief in modern philosophy of management; however the survey results project a blurred picture of the philosophies of management. Further, the managers find themselves "Living in dual world; sanctioned ideology; thus they take hard power or they proclaim that when they are really just firing a few of the lackluster workers".

The study focuses on the scope and limitations of HRD in two different sectors: Government and Private. The philosophy of development and programmes in HRD vary from sector to sector. When we speak of HR, it is not merely the labour and routine physical contribution of HRD in an organization. It encompasses creativity, innovation, sincerity, commitment and a sense of belongingness to the organization on the part of the employees. In this context, we may look back at the scenario of organization in the past. Now the advancing general tendency is more towards concern for good working environment, social responsibility, ethical considerations and ensuring total quality. All these emerging principles of Management are in a way reflected in the dynamic engagement which is an amalgam of essential principles deriving from several theories of Management which have been propounded during the past hundred years.

People enter organization with certain educational, technical and work experience. At the entry point the employees, may not be full-fledged contributors to the growth and development of organizations in terms of production, productivity and management. It is upto the organization to encourage and provide opportunity to the employees in terms of training, motivation and mutually beneficial and healthy interpersonal relations. The HRD of personnel may be initiated at different levels. On the other hand, it could be the initiative and interest on the part of the employees to qualify themselves in respect to what they could maximally contribute to the growth and development of the organization. HRD is a movement towards organizational development. Incidentally the individual employee in the organization once he gets the opportunity of training he benefits. In a sense, HRD primarily is in the interest of the organization. Indirectly the motivated, trained employee derives the benefits in his own enhancement of knowledge, acquiring of new skills and desirable attitudinal change in him. HRD benefits the individual as well as the organization.

When we look at the departments in government either at the central or state level and private sectors, the philosophy, objectives, programmes in respect to HRD differ vastly. In the Indian context or internationally it is the public and private sectors which as a matter of policy lay greater emphasis on upgrading desirable functional knowledge and skills on the part of the employees. Based on a general observation of the government department though, training is taken now as an important activity, the departments concerned do not attach much of importance to the training programmes. It looks rather routine. It is not only the potential and the possibilities on the part of the employees, if the employees are not positively inclined and motivated to avail themselves of the initiatives taken by the organization it will neither contribute to the growth and development of Individual nor organizational progress. Creating work environment, providing good facilities, importance accorded to the individual in the organization, developing a sense of belongingness and ownership on the part of the employees are the positive factors towards HRD. The present study looks at the policy, objectives and programmes of HRD on the part of the organization and the nature and degree of response from the employees. Further, the study also looks into the limitations on the part of the employees in respect to academic qualification at the entry point, potential and interest to move forward in terms of their capabilities and their attitude.

In general, organizations whether of government or private sector lay varied emphasis on training their personnel in view of the present functional and productive needs of the organization, and also the future requirements of the organization. Some organizations carry on routine kind of functions, some always move towards expansion and progressive pace of improving their products and services. Such organizations not only look for advanced and sophisticated machinery but they invest more on enhancing knowledge, developing skills and orientating their employees with desirable attitudes towards working in teams and realizing objectives of the organization. In other words they lay more emphasis on the human factor.

REFERENCES

1. Fred Luthans, *'Organizational Behavior'*, McGraw Hill Irwin Publication, pp., 16-19.
2. Harbison, F. and Myres, C.A., - *'Education., Manpower and Economic Growth'*, Mc. Graw Hill, New York, 1964, pg.2
3. Allen, A. Zall (1966) 'Training Reading Material' supplied by Dr. MCR HRD IAP on 'Human Resource Development' pg. 39.

4. Fowler, 'When Chief Executives Discover HRM', Personnel Management, January 1987. pp. 32-35
5. Daver R.S. (1988) *'Personnel Management and Industrial Relations'.* Vikas Publishing Pvt. Ltd., New Delhi P. 129.
6. Prahalad C.K. and Hamel G. (1990) 'The Core Competence of the Organisation', H.B.R., May-June 1990. pp. 34-36.
7. Venkata Ratnam, C.S (1990), " Integrative approaches to HR function", back ground paper for the National Annual conference of the National Institute of Personal management, Hyderabad, 24 – 27th October
8. William P.A.(1993) *"Strategic Human Resource Management"* The Dryden Press pp 220-221
9. John Purcell, 'Temporary work agencies: here today, gone tomorrow?', British General of Industrial Relations, 4(2): 4 November.
10. Chakraborthy S.K. (1995), "Human Resource Development" Exploring Transformation of Values New ASC Pvt. Ltd. PP. 178-179
11. Mohan Rao (1996) *"HRD in Indian Organisations" selected readings in HRD* by K. Singh, T.V. Rao, B. Nair, Tata Mcgraw Hill Publishing Co. Ltd., 1996; Page 28
12. A.B. Siva Kumar, *"The Hindu Speaks on Management"* – Published by Kasturi & Sons Ltd., 1996. Pages 182 – 186.
13. Ulrich D (1997), The Human Resource Champion: The Next agenda for adding value and delivering results, Boston, MA. Harvard Business School
14. Gratton et al – *'Strategic Human Resource Management*: Corporate Rhetoric and Human Reality' Oxford University.
15. Adopted from Bhatia S.K. (2000), *Personnel Management & Human Resources Management*, 2nd Edition, Deep & Deep Publication Pvt. Ltd. Pp. 3, 29
16. Indu Jain, Times of India, 9th March 2002) http://Spiritualilty.indiatimes.com
17. Prof. E.G. Parameswaran, *"Perspectives on HRD"*, Nilkamal Publications Pvt. Ltd., 2003, Hyderabad. Pages 86 – 105.
18. Prof. Udai Pareek, *"Repositioning HRD: Some Reflections"*, *Perspectives on HRD*, Nilkamal Publications Pvt. Ltd., 2003, Hyderabad. Pages 106 – 114.

19. T.V. Rao & E. Abraham S.J., *HRD Climate in Organisation", Readings in Human Resource Development;* T. V. Rao, Oxford & IBH Publishing Co. Pvt. Ltd., 2004. Pages 36 – 41

20. T.V. Rao & E. Abraham S.J., *"Research in Human Resources Development: Present Trends and Future Directions"*; Readings in Human Resource Development, T. V. Rao, Oxford & IBH Publishing Co. Pvt. Ltd., 2004. Pages 46 – 70.

21. T.V. Rao & E. Abraham S.J., *"Strategies of Developing Human Resources", Readings in Human Resource Development,* T. V. Rao, Oxford & IBH Publishing Co. Pvt. Ltd., 2004. Pages 207 – 228.

22. Adopted from T.V. Rao, *"Readings in Human Resource Development"*, Reprinted from Management in Government, 8(2), 159-176, Oxford & IBH Publishing Co. Pvt. Ltd., 2004.Page 396

23. T.D. Tiwari & M.S. Anuja Thakkar, *"New Dimensions to HRD"* Wisdom publications, New Delhi, 2005 – Page No.13

24. Anil Kumar Singh : Vikalpa – The Journal of Decision Makers, Volume No.30, No.2, April – June 2005 Pages 71 to 78.

3

TRAINING AS A MAJOR CONTRIBUTOR TO HRD

Training of personnel in all fields of development activities has, in the recent past, gained considerable importance. It is a necessary human input for development. The diverse categories of adults who are trained constitute a different audience from that of a school or university. The success of any training programme depends importantly on five factors: the participant (learner), the trainer (teacher), the sponsoring organisations of the participants and the training institute and, the training technology employed. Training essentially is an interaction between the participant and the trainer. Learning very much depends on the climate that is created by the five factors mentioned above.

Training is an essential human resource development activity. It is an investment on people since people are primary in all endeavours in life in making things better. Training is for action, accomplishment, improved performance, managing men and material. It is behaviour to be taught and learnt. The very existence and progress in life in all spheres of life is based on informal and formal training. Training is to meet one's needs and contribute to development. It is well nigh impossible to imagine how life would be minus training.

Man is born with genetically transmitted potential. We may call this as nature and nurturing this biological endowment that takes place right from the infancy upto adulthood and beyond the adult stage is the process of training the individual to fit him to meet his needs and work towards the progress of the community. In development administration, training has become an indispensable necessity with increasing innovations and new ways of accomplishing needs and expectations of people. It is to bring about an extended self in the individual with a concern for the amelioration of all segments of people in the society. Training attempts to bring about an attitudinal change to work towards 'Unto This Last'. We may speak at length about various dimensions of training but it is enough to say that minus training it would be groping in the dark. Training is light that leads you towards continuous betterment of life. Even in the epic period, for instance, in the *Mahabharatha*, the Pandava and Kaurava princes were trained in archery. We cannot imagine a soldier or a general in the army without having undergone training in knowledge and skills related to warfare. They are trained especially in discipline, commitment and determination to serve their country. Training, principally, focuses on three areas: knowledge, skills and attitude. For any effective management, the above three components are essential. One can imagine what happens and the consequences of any performance short of or want of one of the three elements. One may have knowledge in a particular area, but lacks skills to use that knowledge and also inclination to use it (attitude). In another case, one has skill but lacks the needed knowledge and proper attitude. Still in another case, one is positively inclined ready to perform but lacks knowledge and skills. They are to be in the proper functional composition and balance meeting the needs of administration and development. The whole operation in life is learnt behaviour. Training may be called as neo-socialization creating an environment to acquire needed new knowledge, develop requisite skills and also to learn conducive interpersonal behaviour in managing people in getting things done.

Training makes you realize where you are and where you should go and what you should do. It gives you an idea that still miles to go by. Sometimes, training throws some glimmering light on future. Training opens new vistas of knowledge. It makes you feel humble and modest in the area of intellectual exposure. Training is an opportunity for the participant to compare his ideas, views, convictions and knowledge. Training provides means for reflections. Training of personnel assumes greater significance and importance when it comes to development administration. We may think of several analogies likened to the import of training. Training is a kind of intellectual refreshment. Training is just like irrigating a crop periodically. It is reminding and helping people what they are expected to do and how to do. Training invigorates the spirit of commitment. It is drawing strength from each other. Training is sometimes a fine soothing breeze. Sometimes, it opens your eyes, kindles and injects your imagination. It is something like dawn from darkness. Training provides intellectual, social and cultural contacts among the participants and faculty. Training generates flow of new ideas. It is a testing ground for the experience of the participants. Training is going into the open and receiving the sunlight. Learning in groups provides a comparative perspective. It is an opportunity for the personnel to tune with changing times and demands. It tells you that there is something better to learn and apply that learning and make things better.

MULTI-FUNCTIONAL CONTRIBUTIONS OF TRAINING

While the focus of the present book is a critique on training methods, it is relevant to look into functions related to training related to training, the methodology employed in assessment of training methods and the way the training programmes are to be designed depending on the need of the clientele system and the way in which the trainers of the change agents are to instruct, guide motivate, inquire and prepare the trainees from various primary action oriented organisations who are expected to train and enlighten the prospective promoters/change agents working in the relevant areas or fields of action.

Though there is a great deal of writing in respect to function of training, it may not be superfluous and out of place here to briefly touch upon it, since the whole question here revolves around aiding the staff towards better performance wherein training is an investment on people.

Training in a broad sense is a continuous process in life to equip oneself with knowledge, skills and desired patterns of behaviour to be effective as an individual and as a member in the group. Training in a job or activity is again a process of imparting new knowledge and developing skills, attitudes and values in people in order to make them effective and efficient in their job through instruction, practice, demonstration or other techniques either on the job or in a formal training situation.

In view of increase in the on-going activities, introduction of new activities of technical and non-technical nature, growth in the size of organization, induction of new incumbents to a variety of jobs, knowledge and skill demands of new jobs, problems of inefficiency, low productivity and low production, and problems of human relations in the organizational setting, training of the personnel has become a necessity and of late it has assumed greater significance and importance. Training as a remedial measure is also directed towards individual development, competence and efficiency.

Further, the following are the emerging factors necessitating training.

i. Computers

ii. Information Technology

iii. Multinational interaction

iv. Globalization

v. Cultural contact

vi. New Rules and Regulations being brought in

vii. Increased awareness and expectations on the part of the public

viii. Emerging of new ideas, systems, new ways of doing things, and attempts to make things better.

ix. Training as a function in administration

x. Training as a function in development

xi. Training as a necessary input in making things better

xii. Training towards individual growth and development

xiii. Training towards streamlining of organisations

Looked at from any angle irrespective of individual qualifications and capabilities, training has become a necessary component. It has become as a continual process, improving and revamping the human resources, building capabilities in order to ensure satisfactory performance in all endeavours related to administration and rendering services and supplies to the public.

Training in the Context of Professional Staff in Government

None at any level denies the need for a relevant kind of

training. Training does not straightaway imply that there is something deficient and wanting in the individual to be trained. Being professional staff is one thing and competent, effective and efficient is another. Change being a natural and continuous phenomenon in all spheres of life, training has to be a life-long activity. The Government, public and private sector organisations have recognized and emphasized the need for providing training opportunities to the staff for their personal growth and professional competence and better performance.

The need for a particular kind of training may be felt and articulated by a professional staff in respect to the job he/she has to do and the standard of excellence he/she sets for himself/herself. It is not possible always for the individual to come up clearly as to what exactly and precisely he/she needs in terms of training. If it were to be a specific skill as computer use, one could specify, but in areas dealing with socio-economic development and efficient administrative knowledge and skill needs are diverse. Some of these fields in the case of professionals and subject-matter specialists are gray areas seemingly known and unknown. And so, one of the ways to stipulate and recommend the kinds of training that may be provided to the professional staff is to move from the expected, anticipated performance and the end-product of certain comparable excellence on the part of the staff. This is a supervisory and management assessment and decision, based of course on the role of a particular department / organisation or the whole government as a unified system.

Reward Anticipated and Follow-up of Training

Training is not to be taken as an isolated, single-time activity, but as a process of organizational development. It has pre-training and post-training phases. People some times look forward to some rewards, recognition in whatever form it could be after the training and some may consider training itself as a reward.

In order to make the training serve its purpose and to make the participant really benefit from the training for his own development and contribute to departmental objectives, the concerned department may have to do its part.

A Three-Pronged Approach to Training

In consonance with every department / organisation's approach to Human Resource Development in all fields of administrative and socio-economic development, a three-pronged and an integrated approach to training is recommended. This three-pronged approach focuses simultaneously on individual staff's personal growth, inter-personal relations and professional growth in substantive functional areas. Sensitizing the individual, promoting the inter-personal relations and enriching the professional competence would, it is believed, meet the mandates of any organisation. The essential learning situations which go under different nomenclature as seminars, workshops, labs and training course are clustered under three areas referred to above. As shown in the diagram (Please see Training Schema), the course in each cluster has distinct and at the same time unifying characteristics motivating, strengthening and reinforcing the other clusters, thus facilitating knowledge of the self, understanding of and working with others with excellence in one's own respective functional areas.

Duration of Courses

While considering the duration of course, we may have to reckon with three constraints; time, cost and resources. Most of the courses are elastic in their nature. They could be condensed into a few hours and a couple of days or they could be full-length courses. It is the content of the course and also the level of the participants that matter. Duration of the course also depends on the question, whether it is a basic course or a refresher one. In view of the time, and resource constraints, one may have to compromise, sacrifice

TRAINING SCHEMA

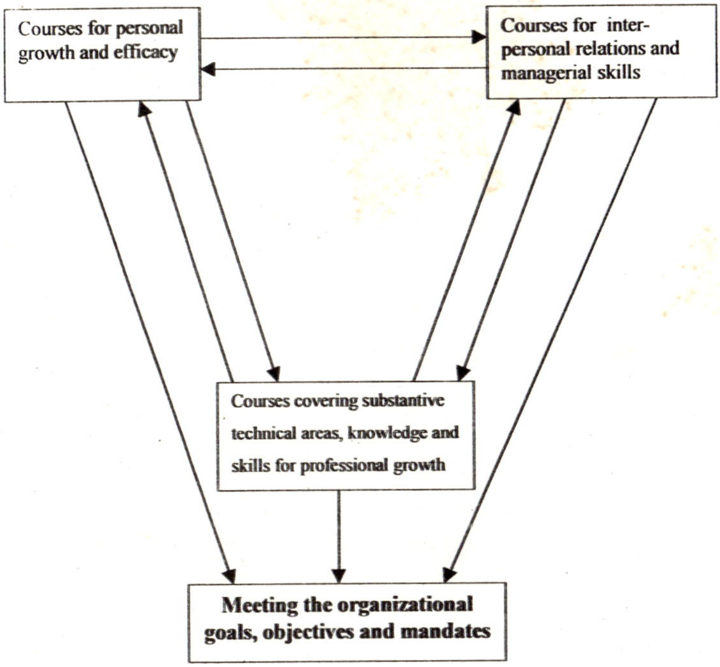

certain content, details, field visits and strike a balance. As Francis Bacon speaks of books: Some books are to be tasted, some are to be swallowed and a few are to be chewed and digested. Similarly, one may think of assigning relative importance to courses and the duration of courses. Training courses are not to be organized for the namesake as a cosmetic touch. Duration or time is one of the significant factors in the impact of a training programme on the participant.

Courses for Personal Growth and Efficacy

Most of the training programmes as mentioned above funnel down to three areas, one dealing with personal growth and development, second focusing on interpersonal relations, and the third covering subject area specializations. As a kind of illustration, we will briefly look into the three types of courses which put together make a wholesome kind of training. One may call this kind of approach an integrated system of training wherein the individual's growth and development and helping him to advance in his area of expertise / specialization and focusing on interpersonal relations which is a significant contributing factor in any kind of activity where the group is involved.

Under three headings, we just include illustrative training programmes that fall within these three areas.

Laboratory for Personal Growth

It is experiential learning and the experience that the participant gains in the small group setting, much of it cannot be explained in words. However, if we were to describe the process, it helps the participants in (a) articulating the un-articulated, (b) making the invisible visible and (c) owning up the disowned and (d) acting the withheld. It is said that growth of a man into being lies by directing his effort to extend these four boundaries in his own life space. The Lab is geared to answer the specific needs for the mobilization of the self and the system in which the individual functions.

Further, the experience-based learning would help individuals and systems to develop socio-psychological infrastructure for anchoring major programmes of change and development. It also enables individuals and systems acquire a realistic appraisal of internal resources and constraints to action and mobilize themselves for alternative action choices which can break the pattern of stagnation and usher in new ways of maximal utilization of human resources in the organization.

Management of Motivation

Motivation is a drive, an urge fuelling and propelling an

individual into action. It is interesting to reflect upon what motivates us and others and how to motivate others. Irrespective of the levels at which individuals operate, superordinate or subordinate, knowledge of factors that motivate people is highly essential. This knowledge facilitates individual satisfaction, promotes understanding of others, fosters healthy inter-personal relations and leads to higher productivity and production. Knowledge of how to motivate your colleagues and subordinates towards coordination and better performance is a psychic tool in management. It is ignorance of this knowledge that leads to misunderstanding, prejudices and miss and under utilization of human resources in an organization.

Communication

Communication assumes various forms and the entire business of human society depends on multiple modes of communication. It plays a basic, essential role in all walks of life. Communication is the ongoing process by which people attempt to share meaning via the transmission of messages. Management constantly is interested in the work performance and the way jobs are done with and through other people in order to achieve the mission, vision, values and goals. Communication provides a common silken thread for all management processes of planning, organizing, leading, controlling and proper coordinating. The management of people through small groups and teams demands continuous communication.

Leadership

Leadership is an important social tool for initiating action, motivating people, mobilizing resources, directing and accomplishing a task. Leadership is task related. It plays the role of guiding and building confidence among people towards better performance. Leadership in different degrees and modes operates in every social system. It is a process of influencing and directing task-related activities of group members. Motivational skills are critical components of leading. It plays a role in organisation and human resources development. One can think of self-inspired leadership and motivated leadership.

Personality Development

Personality is the sum total of ways in which an individual reacts and interacts with others. Heredity and environment may be said as two interacting factors that mould the personality of an individual. Phy ical stature, facial attraction, sex, temperament, muscle composition, reflexes and energy level and biological rhythms are the result of the heredity factor. Environment is related to culture and upbringing. Situational factors influence the effects of heredity and environment on personality. The core trait in a personality of an individual is his character. We have extensive studies on personality formation and behavioral patterns related to each type of personality. Though the foundation is laid in shaping of one's personality in the formative period, it is possible to bring about changes in the attitude or behaviour of an individual especially in his interpersonal relations, mode of working with other people and communication. The study of personality is not only in the interest of one individual but it is essential for any official to understand the personality of others which is a kind of clue for the individual working with another individual or a group.

Courses in Inter-Personal Relations and Managerial Skills[1B]

Right from the family, small group to a large and complex organization, most of the functions are collective. The quality of work, productivity and the harmony that is generated in the work environment depend on mutual understanding and inter-personal relations among the members in the group.

The need for cultivating and fostering healthy, productive relationship in a multi-regional, multi-cultural, multi-lingual and multi-religious personnel composition as obtaining in the governmental organizations is greater. Effective functioning is a learned behaviour and this learning environment is created through training.

Knowledge, skills, methods, techniques, understanding and leadership are the ingredients that are the requisites to work with people and to make people work effectively and efficiently. The courses that are suggested under this cluster focus on building functional inter-personal relations, enhancing supervisory capacity, developing communicative skills and abilities, to introduce and sustain desirable change, managing conflicts incidental to changes in the organization.

Inter-Personal Relations

Public development functions are collective activities that are carried on by a mixed group of people, occupying varied positions of authority and with diverse personal and cultural orientations. To bring about unison in thinking and action amongst such a diverse group is a task wherein you cannot apply force and accomplish things. The only means is to educate and motivate people towards enlightened, cooperative participatory action with personal commitment in accomplishing a public task. The course addresses this issue.

Management of Change and Conflict

Economic and social development implies change and some kinds of change are welcomed and some resisted. It is not only facing change and conflict in the clientele system, but more often we have to face it in the organization itself, when desirable changes are attempted. For instance, one change that is presently attempted in the State of Andhra Pradesh is 'Janmabhoomi' and socio-economic development necessitating streamlining the entire administrative strategies and bringing about changes in the work behaviour of officials in the departments. There is need to prepare people to accept and sustain desirable changes in the organization. The course on Management of Change and Conflict provides an insight into the psychology of human behaviour either favouring or resisting a change phenomenon and the ways to effectively induce a change and handle conflicts that often arise as a result of values, traditions, practices, vested interests and wrong perceptions.

Human Resources Management (HRM)

The personnel in the various organisations and departments of government with their intellectual and psychic endowment constitute the human resources. They are a precious resource. The personnel on their own can and may perform their roles efficiently, but more often they need direction, guidance, appreciation and motivation to do their jobs better. Efficient utilization and management of people in the organization is the responsibility of the management. But people cannot be used as building blocks mechanically. It is an art to work with people and make them more efficient and productive and the HRM course addresses itself to such a task.

Training Methods and Skills (TMS)

It may be said that knowing a thing is knowledge and communicating it is skill. What is attempted in this course is development of communicative skills among professional experts and subject-matter specialists. Some of them who have an aptitude to be trainers could be trained in training methods and skills who could function as resource persons for in-house training programmes and also serve as trainers in respect of training programmes.

This training of trainers (TOT) programme would enhance the training capabilities of the staff to be trained and also sharpen their verbal and non-verbal skills of communication. The TMS course may be organized at least once in a year and senior and middle level staff, around 10 to 15 may be trained who would really be a rich resource and an asset to any Institute.

Performance Appraisal

Performance appraisal is the systematic description of the job relevant to strengths and weaknesses of an individual or a group. It serves two major purposes in organizations. (1) Improving the job performance of employees and (2) Providing information to employees and managers for use in making decisions such as administration, placement, selection-promotion, financial rewards, incentives or compensation etc. The essential purpose in this systematic and periodic appraisal is the accurate measurement of human performance. It attempts to reduce if not to eliminate human bias and prejudice by means of a system that is subject to impartial review and check.

Team Building

Most of the activities in organizations are collective in nature carried on by teams ranging from 8-10, each individual playing a specified role and coordinating with others in carrying out a particular activity. Team members synchronize their efforts towards translating a designed objective. Team building can be within groups or at the inter-group level where activities are inter-dependant. The teams may go by different names such as committees, project teams, self-management teams and task groups. The most vital role of an organization is to build teams and foster them towards accomplishing of organizational tasks.

Supervisory Training

A supervisor may be called a manager in action who often is in close physical contact with the employee. He has a dual task: Get things done by the employees and at the same time guide, train the employees and also keep up their morale. His is to answer the management and also be friendly with his subordinates. His is no easy task. He is to be competent professionally and at the same time effective in human relations. The supervisory training course focuses on making a good supervisor a better supervisor.

Courses for Professional Growth

As the very title of this cluster of courses stands, the selective courses that are included here chiefly focus, the following courses under subject specialization are only illustrative since there are number of subject areas wherein courses could be offered for further advancement in a particular field.

1) Modern Techniques and Computer Applications in Social Research

   As the title describes, the participant in this course will be exposed to he latest techniques including computer aided statistical package in carrying out social research.

2) Project Planning and Implementation

   The course focuses on the information, knowledge, skills and techniques required to plan sound development projects.

3) Poverty Focused Development Planning

   What is called poverty in the economic sense is a complex phenomenon in any society. It has social, cultural and psychic dimensions though economic attribute is visible and usually the one that is looked into. There is what is called culture of poverty. Mere money alone cannot reduce or eliminate poverty. To alleviate one has to work through several intricate and deep-rooted barriers. The approach is through education, skill development, motivation and facilitating the poor to wriggle out from the clutches of poverty. The course tries to open up means towards this end.

4) Programme Planning

It deals with the principles, philosophy and guidelines that one has to bear in mind while planning a development programme. In the set of priorities in programme planning the place of primacy is given to the beneficiary group, who and how many and to what extent they will be benefited.

5) System Analysis for Integrated Systems Management

The course focuses on the inter-connected, inter-dependent and mutually influencing sub-systems in a system of activity. Knowledge of system analysis would help towards effective management and bring about an integrated development economizing the cost of any project.

6) Sustainable Development

The need that we have to address today is not only development, but more importantly sustainable development. This concept of sustainability relates to physical resources, economic structure, technology, environment, social institutions, and the consumption pattern of the people. The course draws attention to all these factors that impinge on sustainable development.

7) Sustainable and Environmentally Sound Development

This course draws the attention of participants to plan sustainable development especially in the fields of agriculture, industry, land and forest use and tourism safeguarding the environment.

8) Management of Agricultural Extension

   Agricultural extension as an applied non-formal education spans from research lab to farm encompassing several layers of administration and line agencies. Managerial aspects are pivotal in delivering of services and goods to the farmers on time in the right way. The course addresses the managerial aspects of agricultural extension.

9) Planning and Promotion of Integrated Area Development

   Area, a district, a sub-district, a region, a tribal or coastal region is the unit of development in this approach. It is a multi-project development in a selected geographic area.

10) Promotion of Self-Employment

    The course looks into several means and ways of promoting self-employment as the basis for income generation leading to minimum quality of life, supported by country case studies.

11) Small Industry Sickness Prevention and Rehabilitation

    Some small enterprises started under pressure of targets, ill-planned, ill-equipped and wrongly located and due to mismanagement or want of finance, raw material, infrastructural facilities and finding no market for the goods and services, fall sick. The course addresses the ways to prevent sickness and rehabilitate the sick enterprises.

12) Small Industry Management Consultancy

    As the title of the course says, it is a specialized field and of a multi-disciplinary nature. It is optional to the industry development staff.

13) Information Storage and Retrieval Systems

    It may be called informatic science highly useful to the librarians and people working in the information centres. It deals with providing accessibility to the users employing the latest techniques.

Relative Importance of Courses

The importance of any training course is dependent on the need felt for it and so, one may accord importance to different courses. The three clusters of courses recommended for the staff, as mentioned earlier, focus on person, group and subject – two courses on personal growth and efficacy, five on inter-personal relations and others on substantive subject technical areas.

Besides the unquestionable and undeniable importance of training provided to the employees, the field study looked into the following factors contributing to HRD and healthy working environment.

a) Work commitment on the part of the employees

b) The work environment

c) Workers participation in formulating and in achieving goals and objectives of the organization.

d) Inter-personal relations

e) Prospects towards career development.

f) Work culture

4

RELEVANCE OF HRM TO HRD

It is to be pointed out here HRD as a factor as an input or raw material and HRM deals with the system of making use of utilizing maximally HRD input for growth and development of an organization. In a real sense HRM may be as twin to and closely associated with HRD. In this context we may briefly look into the way in which HRM utilizes and manages the HRD factor among the employees in an organization.

The concept of Human Resource Management and its historical evolution in terms of its multiple contributions to the organisations and the employees in the organisation deserves a serious examination. The recognition to Human Resource Management was not invented but discovered, appreciated, implemented and evaluated from several organisations and countries gained through trial and error experience. The growth of organisations, increase in the number of employees, diversification of industrial activities, are concerned and sensitive towards maximal utilization of resources or inputs. Organisations over a period of time at the managerial level realized that the efficiency of organisation is largely dependent on effective and sensible use of management of human resources i.e. people employed in the organisations.[1] The global nature of business has made the management and the employees to think, recognize and realize the benefits on both sides, employees and organization.

As mentioned above Human Resource Management has attained the status of a discipline in academic terms, which is used as human tool. This discipline exercises meaningful and standard control in a positive sense over the employees in an organisation. It may also be noted here [2]Human Resource Management is not an anti employee. It is a guiding, motivating, directing force to the employees to meet the objectives and goals of an organisation. In simple terms it is a sensible and meaningful utilization of employees' ideas, skills and knowledge and their talents in meeting the organisational objectives and requirements. In a larger sense it is an education both for the organisation and the employees. [3]Human Resource Management {HRM} as a discipline is growing, expanding and getting standardized based on experience and experimentation by thousands of organisations world over.

[4]Human Resource Management (HRM) is concerned with the 'People' dimension in management. Organisations are managed and staffed by people. Without people, organisations cannot exist. Indeed, the challenge and the opportunity of creating and managing organisations frequently stem from the people–related problems that arise with them. People-related problems, in turn, frequently stem from the mistaken belief that people are all alike, that they can be treated identically. Nothing could be further from the truth. Like snowflakes, no two people are exactly alike, and everyone differs physically and psychologically from every one else. Sitting in a sports arena, for example, will be tall people, short people, fat people, thin people, people in colour, elderly people, young people, and so on. Even within any single physical category there will be enormous variability in psychological characteristics. Some will be outgoing, others reserved, some will be intelligent, others not so intelligent,

some will prefer indoor activities, others outdoor activities. The point here is that these differences demand attention so that each person can maximize his or her potential, so that organisations can maximize their effectiveness, and so that society as a whole can make the wisest use of its human resources.

Since every organisation is made up of people, acquiring their services, developing their skills, motivating them to high levels of performance and ensuring that they continue to maintain their commitment to the organisation are essential in achieving organizational objectives. This is true regardless of the type of organisation – government, business, education, health, recreation, or social action. Getting and keeping good people is critical to the success of every organisation, whether profit or non-profit, public or private.

[5]Those organisations that are able to acquire, develop, stimulate, and keep outstanding workers will be both effective (able to achieve their goals) and efficient (expending the least amount of resources necessary). Those organisations that are ineffective or inefficient, risk the hazards of stagnation or going out of business. Survival of an organisation requires competent managers and workers coordinating their efforts towards an ultimate goal. While successful coordination cannot guarantee success, organisations that are unsuccessful in getting such coordination from managers and workers will ultimately fail.

[6]The evolving role of HRM encompasses an ever-widening scope of responsibilities that contributes more directly to the organisation's bottom line. HRM is an integrated set of managerial functions, not just a collection of techniques. To look at HRM more specifically we have to understand that it is a process consisting of four functions – Acquisition, Development, Motivation and Maintenance of human resources.

We can show those four functions through a diagram:

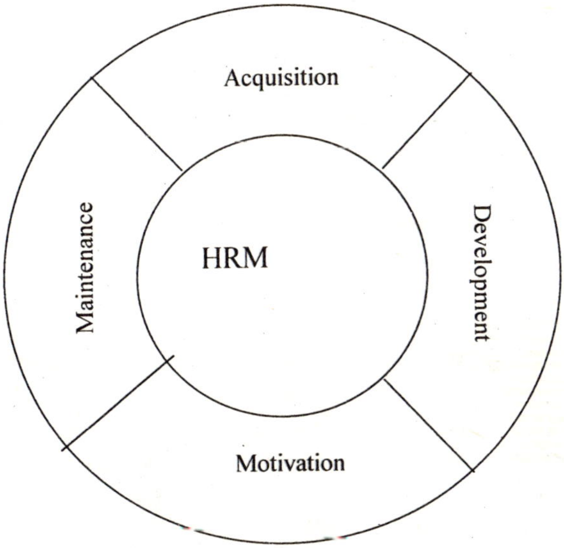

Diagram: 1 - A Model for Four Functions of HRM

HRM Components

Acquisition	Development	Motivation	Maintenance
• Human Resources Planning	• Employee Training	• Job Design	• Safety and Health
• Recruiting	• Management	• Performance Evaluation	• Employee / Labour Relations
• Internal	Development	• Rewards	
• External	• Career Development	• Job Evaluation	
• Employee Socialization		• Compensation / Benefits	
		• Discipline	

The above functions are explained below briefly:

Acquisition Function

The acquisition function begins with planning. Relative to human resource requirements, we need to know where we are going and how we are going to get there. This includes the estimating of demands and supplies of labour (job analysis and human resource planning). Acquisition also includes recruitment, selection, and socialization of employees.

Development Function

The development function can be viewed along three dimensions. The first is employee training, which emphasizes skill development and the changing of attitudes among workers. The second is management development, which concerns itself primarily with knowledge acquisition and the enhancement of an executive's conceptual abilities. The third is career development, which is the continual effort to match long-term individual and organisational needs.

Motivation Function

It begins with the recognition that individuals are unique and that motivation techniques must reflect the needs of each individual. Within the Motivation Function, alienation, job satisfaction, performance appraisal, behavioral and structural techniques for stimulating worker performance, the importance of linking rewards to performance, compensation and benefits administration and how to handle problem employees are reviewed.

Maintenance Function

The final function is maintenance. In contrast to the motivation function, which attempts to stimulate performance, the maintenance function is concerned with providing those working conditions that employees believe are necessary in order to maintain their commitment to the organisation.

Within the confines of the above four functions many changes have occurred over the years. What once was merely an activity to find a warm body to fill a vacancy has become a sophisticated process of finding, developing and retaining the best-qualified person for the job. But this metamorphosis did not occur overnight. It is the result of many changes in management thought, society and the workers themselves.

[7]It may be mentioned here that the emergence of Human Resource Management has provided the focus for a wide-ranging debate concerning the nature of the contemporary employment relationship not only in the United States and Britain, but in many other market economies too. The starting point of this debate is the recognition that the nature of the employment relationship has experienced a series of important changes and adaptations over the past decade which are both significant in themselves and look likely to provide the basis for further development in the medium term. Among the more substantial contemporary changes noted in the Globe are:

- a decline in the proportion of employees in trade unions;
- a decline in the proportion of employees whose pay is set by unionized collective bargaining;
- a reduction in the range of employment issues that are handled collectively coupled with;
- a rise in the range of employment issues that are derived out of franchised employment and a considerable rise in the short – term, part time, contracted out of franchised employment.

The immediate significance of the emergence of Human Resource Management, certainly in the British Context, is to have opened up a vigorous debate about what constitutes the change from traditionally conceived employee management policies to those which are claimed to be derived from a different mix of managerial concerns. Among the more prominent aspects which have been claimed for Human Resource Management are derived from a more focused managerial perspective which is often strategically driven and that it represents a more unified and holistic approach than the 'technical-piecemeal' approach of personnel Management. In this manner Human Resource Management as depicted having an agenda which addresses 'business – related' issues and hereby contribute to the overall success of the organisation in a proactive manner [8]where HRM constitutes a series of integrated decisions that form the employment relations; their quality contributes to the ability of the organizations and the employees to achieve their objectives. While personnel management is depicted as having an agenda set for it by the more mundane requirements of the day.

In one sense, Human Resource Management has become a system comprising the ways & means and dos' & don'ts in understanding effectively, maximally and productively utilizing the Human Resource of every individual employee and coordinating the activities of the employees. It ultimately funneling down to achieving the stipulated aims and objectives of the organisation. [9]These objectives can be achieved in several acceptable ways. This idea, called 'equifinality' which means, there are usually multiple paths to achieve objectives. The key to success is picking the path that best fits the organisation's culture.

Human Resource Management as a discipline cannot be considered as a stereotype one, the ideas and the approaches are there but the wisdom and success lie on the part of the managers or executives who are responsible for managing the human resource of the employees. [10]Human Resource Management contains more diversity and complexity and incorporates such issues as the philosophies of personnel and industrial relations, the professional desire to present the management of employees as a holistic discipline (akin to the inclusive approaches of Accounting and Marketing, for example), and the belief that an integrated management approach can be provided by HRM. An important outcome of this approach is to view some of these traditional components as now irrelevant or outdated and as dealing with problems which typify past, as opposed to current, practice: this is, perhaps, most noticeable in the renaming of functional activities so that Industrial Relations becomes "Employee Relations" and Training becomes 'Employee Development'. HRM as an individual focused developmental model has fostered a culture within personnel management which is categorized as 'cost minimisation' with the individual as the cost which has to be controlled and contained. The logical extent of this model is reached in manpower planning with precise numerical assessments of internal and external demand for and supply of labour.

HRM as a strategic and international function has the advent of Human Resource Management and also brought forward the issue of linkages between the employment of relationship and wider organisational strategies and corporate policies. [11]Strategies include environmental scanning, strategy formulation, strategy implementation, evaluation and control. Historically, the management of Industrial Relations and Personnel has been concerned to cope with either the 'downstream' consequences of earlier strategic decisions or to 'firefight' short term problems which threaten the long-run success of a particular strategy. In these instances the role has been at best reactive and supportive to other managerial functions, at worst a hindrance until particular operational problems were overcome. Further, HRM points to its international potentialities. The employment relationship is materially affected – perhaps even defined – by the national and cultural contexts in which it operates. Thus, variations in national labour markets have given rise to a wide range of employment structures, policies and relationships within the broad definition of market economies. HRM is also capable of providing a managerial approach to the employment relationship that is 'culturally neutral', is derived and sustained from within and organisational boundaries.

[12]In terms of HRM gaining importance in respect to its inputs and action, we may cite here a brief process of change and development from labour relations moving on to personnel management and ultimately emphasizing human resources in organisation. The following graphical figure briefly indicates this movement.

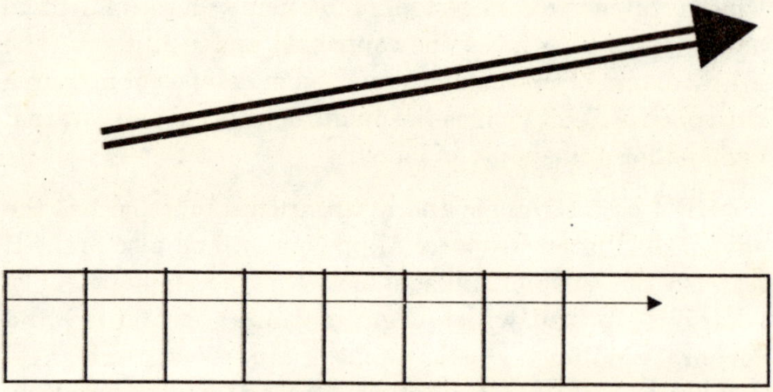

1930	1960	1990
Labour Reiations	Personnel Management	Human Resources

Diagram: 2

Evolution from Labour Relations to Personnel Management

The employee was used as a social tool and the management was only concerned in extracting work from each employee the work that was assigned to him. The workers were recruited through a labour contractor. In many organisations it appears there was no life tenure of guarantee or permanence of job to the individual employees. The management utilized the knowledge and skill that was available with the individual employee. During this period (Labour Relations Period, 1930-1960) there were no avenues/ institutions offering training for further advancement of knowledge, skills and managerial abilities on the part of the employees. The training institutes either of a general professional in nature or training wing either of the government or private concerns were very few and also poorly equipped with resources and faculty in different fields of training. In terms of incentives provided to the employees by the government or private organisations are almost very negligible. The realization of employee development and the care that has to be taken in respect to the employees came rather late. The awakening in respect of employees' importance grew gradually in many of the larger organisations through out the world. The contact and interaction between the top management and the workers felt to increase. These factors gave rise to emergence of Personnel Management.

Evolution from Personnel to HRM

The enlightenment on the part of workers has gradually changed the scenario in the organisations. The day has come where the management has to bend and listen to the workers. In a way, the management has to toe almost the views, ideas and challenges thrown by workers. Of course, the scenario differs from organisation to organisation. Over a period of three decades, because of multiple factors personnel management slowly assumed a greater significance by 1960s.

Personnel departments were once called 'Health and Happiness' departments. The people assigned to deal with personnel issues were often individuals who were passing their time. The personnel department was seen as a place where less productive employees could be placed with minimal damage to the organisation's ongoing operations. Individuals in the personnel department were perceived as those responsible for planning company picnics, vacation schedules and retirement parties. Personnel as an activity, was seen as a necessary but unimportant, part of the organisation.

Yet, as the field of management began to mature, more emphasis was being placed on the workers. Various studies revealed that organising workers for the work they had done could influence their productivity. Workers were becoming more demanding in what they wanted from a job and society, by means of laws and legislation. No longer could the personnel department be treated as a detour on the road to success. Organisations had to hire the best-qualified candidates without regard to race, religion, sex, national or international. The individuals hired needed to be trained to function effectively within the organisation. Further more, once hired and trained, the organisation had to provide a means of continuing the personal development of each employee.

Practices were needed to ensure that these employees maintained their productive affiliation with the organisation. Finally, work conditions have to be established such that the work environment induced workers to stay with the organisation and simultaneously attracted new applicants to the organisation. Thus the importance to HRM evolved.

While discussing the recognition of HRM, it is relevant here that we look into briefly the defined HRM, evolution of the concept of HRM and the differences between the traditional personnel approach and the human resource approach.

HRM Defined

[13]HRM can be defined as a strategic and coherent

approach to the management of an organisations most valued assets – the people working there, who individually and collectively contribute to the achievement of its objectives. A distinction has been made by Storey (1989) between the 'hard' and 'soft' versions of HRM.

Versions of HRM: Hard & Soft

Hard HRM

The hard approach to HRM emphasizes the quantitative, calculative and business-strategies aspects of managing the headcount resource in as 'rational' a way as for any other economic factor. It adopts a business-oriented philosophy that emphasizes the need to manage people in ways that will obtain added value from them and thus achieve competitive advantage. It regards people as human capital from which a return can be obtained by investing judicially in their development. [14]Fombrum et *al* (1984) quite explicitly presented workers as another key resource for managers to exploit .

HRM is based on the business case of a need to respond to an external threat from increasing competition. It is a philosophy that appeals to Management who are striving to increase competitive advantage and appreciate that they must invest in Human Resources as well as new Technology.

The emphasis is therefore on:

- The interests of management
- Adopting a strategic approach that is closely integrated with business strategy;
- Obtaining added value from people by the processes of human resource development and performance management;
- The need for a strong corporate culture expressed in mission and value statements and reinforced by

communications, training and performance management processes.

Soft HRM

The soft model of HRM traces its roots to the human relations school, emphasizing communication, motivation and leadership. [15]As described by Storey (1989) it involves 'treating employees as valued assets, a source of competitive advantage through their commitment, adaptability and high quality (of skills, performance and so on)'. It therefore views employees, as means rather than objects. The soft approach to HRM emphasizes the need to gain the commitment – the 'hearts and minds' of employees through involvement, communications and other methods of developing a high commitment, high trust organisation. Attention is also drawn to the key role of organizational culture.

The focus is on 'mutuality', a belief that the interests of management and employees, can indeed should, coincide. It is therefore a unitary approach. So, organisations are assumed to be 'harmonious and integrated, all employees sharing the organizational goals and working as members of one team'.

It has, however, been observed that 'even if the rhetoric of HRM is soft, the reality is often hard, with the interests of the organisation prevailing over those of the individual'. [16]Research carried out by Gratton *et al* (1999) found out that in the eight organisations they studied, there was a mixture of hard and soft HRM approaches. This suggested to the researchers that the distinction between hard and soft HRM was not as precise as some commentators have implied.

Development of the HRM Concept

Some aspects of the basic philosophy of 'soft HRM' can be traced back to the writings of McGregor (1960) who, even used the terminology 'hard' and 'soft' to characterize forms of management control. McGregor's theory X essentially describes the 'control' model of management as described by [17]Walton (1985), while McGregor's theory Y emphasizes the importance of integrating the needs of the organisation and those of the individual, the principle of mutual commitment, again expressed by Walton.

The full concept of HRM emerged in the mid-1980s against the background of the popularist writers on management who flourished in that decade. These included [18]Peters and Waterman (1982) who produced lists of the attributes that they claimed characterized successful companies. These popular 'school for excellence' writers may have exerted some influence on management thinking about the need for strong cultures and commitment, two features of the HRM philosophy.

The concept of HRM has gone through three stages

1. The initial concepts developed by American writers in the 1980s.
2. The take-up of these comments by British writers in the late 1980s and earlier 1990s who were often sceptical about the reality beyond the rhetoric and dubious about its morality.
3. The assimilation of HRM into traditional personnel management.

The two initial concepts of HRM have been christened by [19]Boxall (1992) as the 'matching model' and the 'Harvard framework'.

The matching model of HRM

One of the first explicit statements of the HRM concept was made by the Michigan School (Fombrum *et al* 1984). They held that HR systems and the organisation structure should be managed in a way that is congruent with organizational strategy (hence the name 'matching model'). They further explained that there is a human resource cycle (adaptation of which is illustrated in Diagram 3), which consists of four generic processes or functions that are performed in all organisations. These are:

1. *Selection* – Matching available human resources to jobs.
2. *Appraisal* – Performance management
3. *Rewards* – 'the reward system is one of the most under – utilized and mishandled managerial tools for driving organisations performance'. It must reward short-as well as long-term achievements, bearing in mind that 'business must perform in the present to succeed in the future'.
4. *Development* – Developing high-quality employees

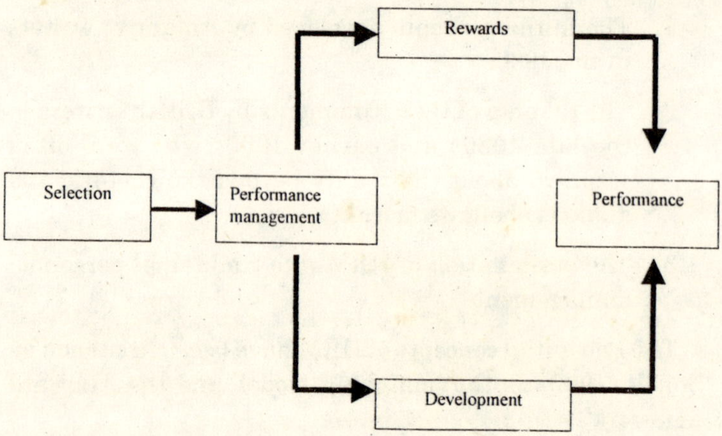

Diagram: 3

[20]Fomburm *et al* suggested that the HR function should be linked to the line organisation by providing the business with good HR databases, by ensuring that senior managers

give HR issues as much attention as they give to other functions, and by measuring the contribution of the HR function at the strategic, managerial and operational levels.

The Harvard framework

The other founding fathers of HRM were [21]Beer *et al* (1984) of the Harvard School who developed what Boxall (1992) calls the 'Harvard framework'. This framework is based on the belief that the problems of historical personnel management can only be solved.

When general managers develop a viewpoint of how they wish to see employees involved in and developed by the enterprise, and of what HRM policies and practices may achieve those goals. Without either a central philosophy or a strategic vision – which can be provided only by general managers – HRM is likely to remain a set of independent activities, each guided by its own practice tradition.

Beer and his colleagues believed that 'Today, many pressures are demanding a broader, more comprehensive and more strategic perspective with regard to the organisations human resources'. These pressures have created a need for 'a longer-term perspective in managing people and consideration of people as potential assets rather than merely a variable cost.' They were the first to underline the tenet that HRM belongs to line managers.

They also stated that: 'Human resource management involves all management decisions and action that affect the nature of the relationship between the organisation and its employees – its human resources'.

The Harvard school suggested that HRM had two characteristic features: 1) line managers accept more responsibility for ensuring the alignment of competitive strategy and personnel policies; and 2) the personnel function has the mission of setting policies that govern how personnel activities are developed and implemented in ways that make them more mutually reinforcing.

The Harvard framework as modeled by Beer *et al* is shown in Diagram 4.

According to Box all (1992) the advantages of this model are that it

- Incorporates recognition of a range of stakeholder interests;
- Recognizes the importance of 'trade-offs', either explicitly or implicitly, between the interests of owners and those of employees, as well as between various interest groups;
- Widens the context of HRM to include 'employee influence', the organisation of work and the associated question of supervisory style;
- Acknowledges a broad range of contextual influences on management's choice of strategy, suggesting a meshing of both product-market and socio-cultural logics;
- Emphasizes strategic choice – it is not driven by situational or environmental determinism.

The Harvard model has exerted considerable influence over the theory and practice of HRM, particularly in its emphasis on the fact that HRM is the concern of management in general rather than the personnel function in particular. Walton (1985), also of Harvard, expanded the concept by emphasizing the importance of commitment and mutuality.

The new HRM model is composed of policies that promote mutuality – mutual goals, mutual influence, mutual respect, mutual rewards, and mutual responsibility. The theory is that policies of mutuality will elicit commitment, which in turn will yield both better economic performance and greater human development.

The commitment model of human resource management is associated with the concept of soft HRM referred to earlier.

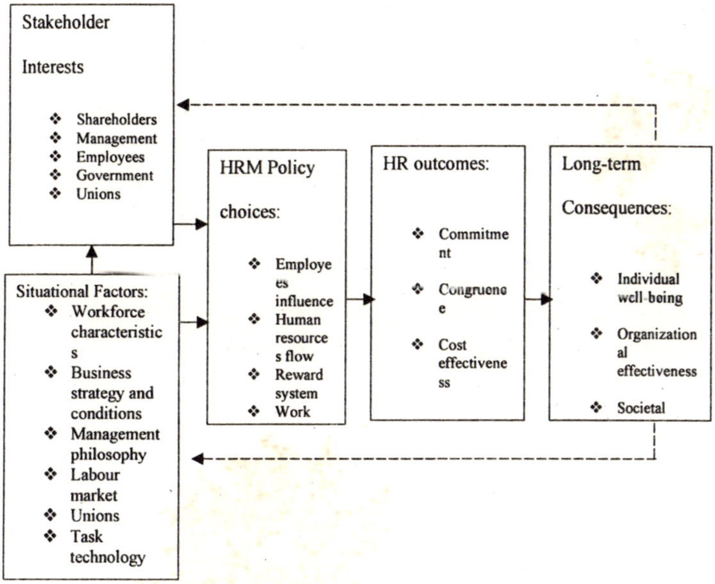

Diagram 4: The Harvard Framework for Human Resource Management.

Here we look into briefly the differences between the strategic Human Resource Approach and the Traditional Personnel Approach.

[22]Differences Between the Strategic Human Resource Approach and The Traditional Personnel Approach

Traditional Personnel Approach	Human Resource Approach
Planning & Strategy Formulation	
• Is involved in operational planning only.	• Participates in formulating organisational strategic plan and aligning HR functions with company strategy.
Authority	
• Medium status and authority (e.g. Personnel Director)	• High Status and authority (e.g. Vice President for Human Resources)
Scope	
• Concerned primarily with hourly, operational, and clerical employees.	• Concerned with all managers and employees.
Decision Making	
• Makes operational decisions only	• Participates in strategic decisions
Integration	
• Moderately integrated, at best, with other organisationalfunctions	• Fully integrated with other organisational functions, such as marketing, finance, legal and production.
Coordination	
• Coordinates a subset of human resource activities	• Coordinates all human resource activities.

One could see as indicated above the gradual shift of rules and emphasis in respect to personnel management ultimately resulting human resource management.

[23]Further, we could also see the changing responsibility and functions of certain roles in the organisations in the recent past and now.

Until Recent Times		Current Time
Hierarchy	ORGANIZATION	Network
Self-Sufficiency	STRUCTURE	Interdependencies
Security	WORK EXPECTATIONS	Personal growth
Homogeneous	WORKFORCE	Culturally diverse
By Individuals	WORK	By teams
Domestic	MARKETS	Global
Cost	COMPETITIVE ADVANTAGE	Time
Profits	FOCUS	Customers
Capital	RESOURCES	Information
Board of Directors	GOVERNANCE	Varied constituents
Affordability	QUALITY	No compromises
Autocratic	LEADERSHIP	Inspirational

One could see the interesting and gradual evolution of HRM maximally utilizing and managing physical, material, monetary and human resource to the benefit of employer organisations and employees. It is very interesting growth and we may say that it is likely to reach an appreciable level of standard and sophistication. All for the benefit of man.

It may be pointed out that HRM differs from Human Resource Development in terms of its role. The HR function is all encompassing and includes HRD and more. It is more proactive and change-oriented and needs competencies of a different nature from what the traditional personnel function required. As we have seen already that the traditional personnel function had been more of a maintenance function with very little growth focus. [24]The modern HR function has HRD at its core. HRD is its soul, as Udai Pareek once put it in a talk at the National Institute of Personnel Management in 1978 on 'Personnel Management in Search of a Soul'. The HR function, as it has evolved in India, consists of three main sub-functions: HRD, Industrial Relations and Worker Affairs; and Human Resource Administration. All the above functions constitute Human Resource Management.

HRM in a sense may be considered a genus while HRD is a significant species emerging from HRM.

REFERENCES

1. Nabaghana Pany & Ashok Kumar Rath, 'Emerging role of HRM in Changing Business Scenario', Paper presented at the XXXII National Convention of Indian Society for Training and Development, January 17-19, 2002, Hyderabad, Managing the ever changing organisation, pp. 115-124.
2. Sikula Andrew F. & John F. McKenna, *The Management of Human Resources*, John Wiley, New York, 1984, Pg. 8.
3. M.M. Bagali, 'Employee Empowerment: Renaissance Strategies for creating high performance organisation', Paper presented at the XXXII National Convention of Indian Society for Training and Development, January 17-19, 2002, Hyderabad, Managing the ever changing organisation,Pg. 102.
4. Pareek: Uday and T. V. Rao, *'Designing and Managing HR Systems'*, Oxford & IBH Publishing Company, New Delhi, 1981, pp. 9,10.
5. Rao T.V. & D.F. Pereira, *'Recent experiences in Human Resources Development,* Oxford & IBH Publishing Company, New Delhi, 1981, Pg.5.

6. David A. Decenzo & Stephen P. Robbins, *Personnel / Human Resource Management*, Prentice Hall of India Private Ltd., New Delhi, 1996. pp. 4 - 24
7. Ian Beardwell and Len Holden, *Human Resources Management*, Macmillan Ltd., 1996. pp. 4 - 7
8. George T. Milkovich & Johri W. Boudreau, *'Human Resource Management*, Chicago, Irwin, 1997, Pg. 2.
9. William B. Werther, Jr. & Keith Davis, 'Human Resources and Personnel Management, McGraw Hill, 1994, Pg. 52.
10. Ian Beardwell and Len Holden, Op. Cit., Pg. 8.
11. Donals F. Harvey, Strategic Management and Business Policy, 2nd Ed., Columbus, Merrill Publishing, 1988, Pg. 5.
12. Professor Janis Langstaff, Reading material on Human Resource Management prepared by MIM, pg. 9.
13. Storey, *'Management of Human Resources*' Oxford, Blackwell, 1989, pp 42-45
14. Fombrum, Tichy, N.M and Devanna, M.A, *'Strategic Human Resource Management'*, New York, Wiley, 1984, pp32 - 38
15. Storey, Op. Cit., Pg. 46
16. Gratton,et al, *'Strategic HRM : Corporate Rhetoric and Human Reality'*, Oxford University Press, 1999, Pg 11
17. Walton, 'From control to commitment in the work place' Harvard Business Review, March-April 1985, pp 77-84
18. Peters and Waterman, 'Describing the Best Companies in search of excellence of H.R. Strategy, 1982, pg 128
19. Boxall, P; Strategic Human Resource Management: Beginnings of a New theoritical sophistication, Human Resource Journal, 2(3), 1992, pp. 60-79
20. Fombrun, Op. Cit., Pg.42
21. Beer et al, 'Human Resource Management : A general Managers Perspective, New York, The Free Press
22. Professor Janis Langstaff Op. Cit.,pg. 24.
23. Warne F. Cascio, *Managing Human Resources*, McGraw Hill, 1998. pp.8– 9.

24 Prof. T.V. Rao, HRD Audit, A Division of Saga Publications, 1999, Pg. 27.

5

PROFILES OF SELECTED ORGANIZATIONS FOR THE STUDY

The philosophy, principles, objectives, goals and the ways of administering and accomplishing tasks in Government administrative system and private organizations of management defer in several areas in terms of elements and in terms of degrees. Of course whether it is small or large, private or Government certain common approaches or elements are indispensable both in respect to government administrative system and private organizations. The present study attempted the way in which HRD is recognized, importance accorded and performance rewarded in a Government administrative system and a private organization. The present study also attempted a comparative perspective in respect to the Department of Industries in Andhra Pradesh and a private manufacturing and servicing organization located in the same state. The main purpose in the study was to know the kind or uniformity, similarity and diverse differences and degrees of emphasis accorded to the employees in both the selected samples. In this context, it is relevant to provide some details in respect to the two sectors

Private organisations emerge as a profit making business entity and also with an objective to render service to the public and some of the private organizations are altruistic and philanthropic oriented. The private organisations may be owned by an individual, a family, or a couple of partners as a Unit of Management. As mentioned above, the primary objective of private organisations is profit making and incidentally it may meet or it meets the needs of the public in terms of commodities and services. Private organisations have a clear cut vision, philosophy and strategies and objectives in serving the public. Though profit and popularity sometimes may be their primary concern and objective, most of the private organisations have been and are innovative in their approaches, planning, organisation of their systems and carrying out the activities.

When we look at the private organisations irrespective of their size, they enjoy relatively a great amount of freedom and choice in terms of policy, organisation, expansion, salary structure, benefits to the employees, dividend to the shareholders rendering of some philanthropical services to the public, recruitment and administering the whole system in the organisation. They are not burdened heavily with restrictions. The Management in private organisations enjoy benefits through business of the organisation, keeping the employees as actively participating individuals, developing a sense of ownership on the part of the employees in the organisation. What we call 'bureaucracy' is far less comparatively with the Government Departments. In Government departments, we have a long chain of communication and the hierarchy also is lengthy. Any programme to be implemented is a long drawn affair compare to private organisations.

We may not simply highlight the salient features, merits and significant characteristics of private organisations compared to the system that operates in Government departments. They are free in several aspects in terms of the essential goods and services but within the boundaries of law that prevails. The private organisations learn and draw strength sometimes from the success and failures of the government departments. But unfortunately, the bureaucracy in the government system seldom learn lessons from private organisations and inspired by the better ways of rendering service to the public with high degree of response, readiness and highly accountable and answerable to the public. The private organisation always try to feel the pulse or the reaction or the level of satisfaction on the part of the clientele. It may be again emphasized here that the public responses and the level of satisfaction are the resource and asset for the private organisation. No private organisation can ignore or be indifferent to the consumers. The private organizations in their growth and development are sensitive to the feelings, tastes and preferences on the part of the consuming public. It does not mean that the government departments are insensitive and indifferent to the needs and expectations on the part of the public. The Government administration is not business and profit oriented and it supposed to look into the welfare and well being of the people. Though it enjoys certain powers, it is burdened with a circuitous multilevel bureaucratic set up.

Private organisations emulate readiness to change to improve upon and do not show any inhibition in accepting failure all the time comparing with progressive organisations and normally readiness to accept new technology when it is affordable. These tendencies and characteristics in general are seldom and sometimes quiet minimal in Government administrative systems.

The challenge for private organisations is survival, profit, good name and popularity in the field of industrial products and services. In respect to Government Departments there is no competition and internal departments' rivalry. One may go in for ranking of States in the country in respect to achievements in certain fields of administration and development. Normally, various departments at the union and state level do not vie with each other in respect to the standard of performance and achievement. A private organisation more often is a kind of hidden system but whereas the administration in Government Departments is relatively an open system. In respect to private organisations the dominant principle and value is trade, commitment, profit, individual and organisational survival. In a larger sense, interpersonal relations, exchange of views, personal guidance, instructions towards better performance and productivity is more in private organisations.

The survival, growth and development of private organisations depends on their innovativeness, creative leadership, responsibility and accountability on the part of every member in the organisation. Depending on the size of the organisation every individual has a sense of belongingness to the organisation whereas in the departments of the government this is almost rare. It is not a question of comparing private organisations with that of government departments, but it depends on the set up, structure, functions, aims and objectives in respect to private organisations and government departments.

Here we may raise a question whether it is the private organisation which draw lessons from the government departments or the other way. One may have to sincerely respect and adopt "Rigveda" LET NOBLE THOUGHTS COME TO US FROM EVERY SIDE. Often we find private organisations watch and look for any profitable lessons that they may learn from the government administrative system. But one seldom find the officials in the government departments learning new effective methods of administration ways towards increase productivity and rendering of quality services to the public by the private organisations.

Amara Raja Batteries is a manufacturing unit where as the Department of Industries at the state level caters to the promotional activities in respect to small scale, medium and major enterprises in the state.

Amara Raja Batteries in a larger sense is a business enterprise but at the same time it renders service to the variety of organizations. But the department of Industries in India and world over is a promotional agency stimulating, guiding, motivating, providing testified blue prints for starting mini and medium enterprises based on the resources available, needs and marketing demands at present and in the future.

Keeping in view the characteristics, functions, commitment, objectives, philosophy or policy motivating the private organizations and the government departments for the present study "HRD in Government and Private Sectors: A Comparative Study" the researcher has chosen Amara Raja Batteries and the department of Industries at the State level in Andhra Pradesh.

Before taking up the analysis of HRD in these two units it is better to have a brief background and idea of these two units by having a glance at their profiles.

A BRIEF PROFILE OF AMARA RAJA BATTERIES LIMITED (AMARON)

Sri Ramachandra N. Galla, a non-resident Indian (NRI) now settled in India is the main promoter. He is a post graduate engineer with over 16 years experience in power systems as an electrical engineer in Nuclear and conventional source power generating stations across the USA. Mr. Galla went to USA after obtaining degrees from S.V. University, Tirupati & Roorkee University. He holds an M.S. Degree in system science from Michigan State University. After his return to India, he promoted along with Andhra Pradesh Electronics Development Corporation (APEDC). a Rs.2 crore unit – Amara Raja Power Systems Ltd. – for the manufacture of uninterrupted power supply systems (UPS), Battery Chargers, D.C. power supplies & static inverters. For the year ending 31st March, 2002 this unit achieved a sales turnover of Rs.188 Crores and earned a cash profit of Rs.18 Crores. The co-promoter Smt. Aruna Kumari Galla is a diploma holder in computers and has worked in USA.

Amara Raja is a company with commitment to achieve excellence in all its activities, by employing latest technology and with a clear understanding of current power back-up requirements.

History of the Company

Amara Raja Batteries Limited (ARBL) also known as Amaron was established in the year 1985 as private limited company and then converted into public limited company in the year 1990. The company is currently poised on a healthy growth curve and ended the Financial Year 2001 – 02 with a turnover of around 200 crores.

Amara Raja Batteries has a strategic tie up with Johnson Control Inc. of the USA who owns 26% stake in this company. Johnson Controls is a Fortune 500 company and also is the largest manufacturer of lead acid batteries in North America and a leading global supplier to major automobile manufacturers and industrial customers.

Amara Raja has demonstrated its commitment to offer optimum system solutions of the highest quality. And has become the largest supplier of standby power systems to core Indian utilities such as the Indian Railways, Department of Telecommunications, Electricity Boards and major power generation companies. Extensive plans have been charted out for the future, wherein the company undertakes to become the most preferred supplier for power back-up systems.

Amara Raja has always offered time tested world-class technology and processes developed on international standards – be it high integrity Valve Regulated Lead Acid (VRLA) systems like Power Stack and Power Plus or the recently launched high performance UPS battery – KOMBAT and Amaron hi-life automotive batteries that are products of the collaboration efforts of engineers at Johnson Controls Inc. and Amara Raja.

Amara Raja Batteries Limited comprises of two major divisions viz., Industrial Battery Division (IBD) and Automotive Battery Division (ABD).

Industrial Batteries Division (IBD)

Amaraja Raja has become the benchmark in the manufacture of industrial batteries. India is one of the largest and fastest growing markets for industrial batteries in the world and Amara Raja is leading the front, with an 80% market share for standby VRLA batteries. It is also having the facility for producing plastic components required for industrial batteries.

Incorporation

ARBL is the first company in India to manufacture VRLA Batteries (S.M.F.). The company has set up Rs.1920 Lakhs Plant in 18 acres in Karakambadi Village, Renigunta Mandal.

Amara Raja Batteries Limited was established in the year 1985 as Private Limited and then it has been shaped into Limited Company with the advent of GNB Industrial Battery Co. U.S.A. for manufacturing sealed Valve Regulated Lead Acid Storage Batteries (VRLA).

Capacity: The actual installed capacity of IBD is 4,00,000 cells per annum and its capacity utilization reached 3,25,000 cells per annum in the year 2005.

Automotive Battery Division (ABD)

Incorporation

Amaraja Raja Batteries Limited inaugurated a new

automotive plant at Karakambadi in Tirupati on September 24th, 2001. This plant is a part of the most completely integrated battery manufacturing facility in India with all critical components, including plastics sourced in-house from existing facilities on-site. This gives Amara Raja complete control over inventory and product quality. In this project, Amara Raja's strategic alliance partners Johnson controls, USA have closely worked with their Indian counterparts to put together the latest advances in manufacturing technology and plant engineering. It is also having the facility for producing plastic components required for automotive batteries. On the whole it provides employment around 1,340 people.

Capacity

With an existing production capacity of 5,00,000 units of automotive batteries, the new Greenfield plant will now be able to produce 1 million batteries per annum. This is the first phase in the enhancement of Amara Raja's production capacity in which the company has invested Rs.45 crores.

Major Customers of ARBL

ARBL has prestigious clients like FORD, General Motors, Daewoo Motors, Mercedes-Benz, Daimier Crysler, Maruti Udyog Ltd., Telecom, Railways, Power & Premier Auto Ltd. Recently acquired a preferential supplier alliance with Ashok Leyland, Hindustan Motors, Telco, Mahindra & Mahindra and Swaraj Mazda. The company entered the replacement battery segment with the launch of Amaron Hi-life auto batteries.

Culture & Environment

- Amara Raja is putting in place a number of HRD initiatives to foster a spirit of togetherness and a culture of meritocracy and Involves employees at all levels in building organizational support plans and in evolving vision for the organization.

- Encourages initiative and growth among young talented employees. It allows the organization to develop innovative solutions.
- Benchmark pollution control measures, energy conservation measures, waste reduction schemes, massive greenbelt development programs, employee health monitoring and industrial safety programs have already helped us take our environment management program further.
- Amara Raja now secured the ISO-14001 certification in the year 2002 (evidence of our concern for the world around us and in which our children will live).

Quality Policy

Our aim is to achieve customer satisfaction through the collective commitment of our employees in design, manufacture and marketing of reliable power systems, batteries, allied products and services.

We believe that the commitment of our employees is primary for our quality goals. We will train, motivate and involve employees, at every level, to achieve our aim.

The commitment to quality will be demonstrated by confirming to ISO-9001: 1994 quality system standard/QS-9000: 1998 quality system requirements.

Environment Policy

As a good corporate citizen, at Amara Raja is committed to enrich the quality of life of its employees, customers and community at large by minimising impacts on the environment in all its activities relating to design, manufacture and marketing of Batteries, Power Systems, allied products and services.

To fulfil the above commitment, it shall strive to:

- ➢ Comply with applicable environmental legislation's and regulations.
- ➢ Adopt programmes, for reducing pollution and conservation of natural resources.
- ➢ Ensure continual improvement in environment performance through effective environmental management system.

It initiated measures to enhance environmental awareness amongst its employees and its business partners, for achieving above objectives.

This commitment to environment protection will be demonstrated by conforming to environmental management system requirements, specified in ISO-14001: 1906 standard.

Non-smoking zone

Keeping in mind the health of all the employees, smoking is strictly prohibited at any time in the factory premises.

Employee Training & Development

Once an applicant is selected by the company as a member of its personnel, places him in the right job and provides him with training and development facilities needed for him to fit the present job as well as the future career chalked out for such individual.

Induction

Induction is an important initial investment "Amara Raja" makes in an employee. It provides the opportunities to settle down and understand the company as an entity in its totality. It will provide with an insight of who's who in the company. It makes the new entrants to know about the product and technology, the general rules and facilities applicable to them. Induction programme as a means to lay the foundation of a long lasting relationship with the employees. Human Resources Department (HR) is looking after the Training & Development activities.

Employee Welfare

The employee measures taken up in the organisation are:

Dispensary

The Dispensary caters to the need of 100 people everyday. For dispensary there is one full time medical officer, one lab technician and two trained nurses dedicated to give on time service to the employees.

Dispensary is constructed with all facilities. For emergency cases there is an ambulance also. The medicines are supplied free of cost with free consultancy. The doors of the dispensary are open always to meet all emergencies by having its Medical Officer and para medical staff residing in the campus.

Transport facilities

Company provides transportation for employees at subsidized rates. The ARBL provides subsidized transport facilities for all commuting employees. About 350 employees get benefited.

Cafeteria

The new cafeteria building has been constructed for the benefit of 1500 + employees and ARBL does not discriminate cadre, category of employees in its cafeteria services. In fact it also feeds 500 + indirect employees every day. Since the factory is located at a far away place from city, ARBL decided to go ahead with such generous measures.

The company provides subsidised food at 50%. ARBL provides the following services without charging the consumer's (a) Labour (b) Electricity (c) Utensils (d) Fuel (e) Cleansing Material (f) Wear and tear of building and furniture.

Bank facility

The State Bank of India, Settipalli has been requested to set up their extension counter at Karakambadi for the benefit of public as well as Amara Raja employees. The ARBL has constructed a beautiful spacious building for the bankers to start their operations. Accordingly the bank has started its operations.

The ARBL provides electricity, water and sanitary facilities. ARBL has spent about Rs.14,43,000/- towards the construction of bank building.

Residential Complex for employee families and hostel for bachelors:

ABRL has built its residential complex at a cost of Rs.1, 16,81,000/-. Where about 150 families got, and 250 bachelor employees are provided accommodation. The family and bachelor dwellers are provided with certain amenities like 24 hours medical, ambulance, consumers stores etc. A public transport bus also being operated to the township.

Township Amenities Centre

An amenities centre consists of all sorts of shops and service centres including laundry, hairdressing, meat stall, fast food centre, vegetable and milk booth, telephone booth.

To promote the co-operation concept ARBL has encouraged its employees to set up a co-operative consumer stores with a share capital of Rs.5,00,000/-.

The commodities are served on no profit basis against 1-Month credit. The services included satellite TV channel and LP Gas distribution.

Primary School for employee's children

The Primary school has been started in the year 1994 with an ideology to provide education to the children of employees, free of cost, with 14 children. Now the school has 144 pupils with 7 Teachers and a Principal.

In the year 1999 the ARBL has constructed a sophisticated and state of art designed school building complex with playground etc., very close to the Township.

Recreation club for employees

To create healthy avocation to the bachelor employees of the ARBL, the company has established a recreation centre very close to the hostel with an investment of Rs.1,00,000/-, besides an annual expenditure of Rs.50,000/-. About 250 employees got benefited out of it.

Core Values

- Work with integrity
- Customer satisfaction
- Effective employee selection, employee development, motivation & recognition
- Improvement & innovation in every element of our business
- Safety and the environment

Mile Stones of the Company

Year		Mile Stone
1997	-	100 crores turnover
1997	-	ISO- 9001 accredition
1999	-	QS- 9000 accredition

Awards

The awards received by this organization include:

1. "The Spirit Of Excellence"—Award by Academy of fine arts, Tirupati.

2. "Best Entrepreneur of the year 1998"—Award by Hyderabad Management association, Hyderabad.
3. "All Round Performance In Industrial Activity Including Promotion/ Expansion Effort" in the state for the year 1997-98—Award by Federation of Andhra Pradesh chamber of Commerce and Industry (FAPPCI), Hyderabad.
4. "Industrial Economist Business Excellence Award"—1999—Award by the Industrial Economist, Chennai.
5. Excellence Award"—by Institute of Economic Studies(IES), New Delhi on 29th April 1999 at New Delhi.
6. "Udyog Rattan Award"—by Institute of Economic Studies, New Delhi.
7. "Excellence in Environment Management"—by Andhra Pradesh Pollution Control Board, on 5th June 2002 at Hyderabad.
8. 5'S' Excellency Award by CII on December 2005.

The tremendous fast progress and expansion of the organization for last two decades is highly a motivating factor for employees of the organization. As contributors to this phenomenal achievement, they feel proud of their accomplishment and this pride itself is a significant factor contributing to HRD.

Now let us have an insight into the profile of the Department of Industries Government of Andhra Pradesh.

A BRIEF PROFILE OF THE DEPARTMENT OF INDUSTRIES, GOVERNMENT OF ANDHRA PRADESH

Since we are dealing with Department of Industries in Government Sector it is relevant to have an insight in to the brief background and functions of the Department of Industries at the State level.

Origin of the Industries Department

The Industries Department at Hyderabad was formed in the year 1926 by the erstwhile Nizam's Government. The department then consisted of a Secretary to Government and a Director, Dept. of Commerce & Industry. They were assisted by three senior officers' viz., an Industrial Engineer, a Textile Expert and a Deputy Director with other supporting officers and staff. An engineering wing was created and the Industrial Engineer was appointed to give approval for the factory and the boiler layouts. A textile wing was created with the Textile Expert to look after the development of textile industry and also to look after the welfare of spinners and handloom weavers. The Deputy Director was kept in charge of cottage and artisan based industries and handicrafts.

With the outbreak of the Second World War, many steps were taken for the development of Industries in the Hyderabad State. The first step in this direction was the formation of an Industrial Corporation partly financed by the Government and partly by the other agencies, for the manufacture of heavy chemicals, sheet glass and glassware, glucose, casein and plastics. With a view to stimulate industrial activity, a Scientific and Industrial Research Board was constituted for the promotion of industries based mainly on the indigenous and locally available raw materials.

The Department passed through different phases of transformation from a regulatory department to that of a Developmental Agency. After the formation of Andhra Pradesh State, the Industries Department was attending the following functions.

- Works pertaining to boring and drilling of wells.
- Weights and Measures

- Development of Handicrafts, Cotton, Wool and Sericulture based Industries.
- Collecting Industrial Data and Statistics.
- State Director of Industries as the Chief Purchasing Officer for all the State Government Departments.

Functions attended by Industries Department

The small industries development programme commenced only towards the end of the First Five Year Plan (1955-56). The following Centrally sponsored programmes were taken up during the first to fifth plan period.

1. Industrial Estates programme
2. Loans under the State Aid to Industries Act
3. Service Schemes
4. Commercial schemes
5. Common service facility schemes
6. Service-cum-commercial schemes
7. Subsidy on supply of power
8. Industrial cooperatives

Industrial Estates

The principal objectives of the Industrial Estate programme were:-

- To encourage the growth of Small Scale Industries.
- To shift small scale industries from congested urban areas to estate premises with a view to increase their productivity.
- To achieve decentralized industrial development in small towns and large villages.

- To encourage the growth of Ancillary industries in the townships surrounding major industrial undertakings, both in Public and Private Sectors.

Further, it looks into and promotes

- Rural Industries Projects (RIPS):
- Sericulture Activities:
- Leather Tanning & Production Centres:
- Handicrafts Schemes:
- Schemes run by Research and Design Centre:
- Other Training Centres:
- Production Centres & Training Centres under Employment Schemes:

District Industries Centres

In accordance with the New Industrial Policy statement made in December 1977 by the Govt. of India, one District Industries Centres (DICs) was sanctioned for each district to deal with all requirements of small and village industries. The State Government sanctioned 11 DICs vide G.O.Ms.No.761 Industries and Commerce (SSI) dated 3.10.1978, 3DICs vide G.O.Ms.No.481 Industries and Commerce (SSI) Department dated 21-6-1979 and 8 DICs vide G.O. Ms.81 Industries and Commerce (SSI) Department dated 13-2-1981. Soon after the formation of District Industries Centres, additional posts were created as per the pattern suggested by the Government of India and the functions were redefined among the functionaries in the DIC. The State Government with a view to have a uniform staffing pattern among all the District Industries Centres, rationalized the staffing pattern in each district and created Growth Centres and Inspection Wing duly fixing the head quarters and shifted the non-plan posts, along with the persons to

Growth Centres in order to cope up with the work load especially in tiny/decentralized sector in the interest of rural development.

The Development Commissioner (SSI) Govt. of India informed that as per the decision of National Development Council, the District Industries Centres scheme was transferred to the State sector from 1994-95 onwards since then no provision was made by the Govt. of India in the budget of the office of the Development Commissioner (SSI) in this regard. The Departmental Clearance Committee in its meeting held on 28.5.1995 have decided to reorganize the District Industries Staff pattern by reducing the staff strength and also to merge the Growth Centres Offices with District Industries Centres in order to reduce the plan expenditure and to improve the efficiency.

District Industries Centres Programmes are

- Loan Assistance Programmes:
- Rural Artisan Complexes:
- Mini-Industrial Estates for Scheduled Castes & Scheduled Tribes
- Rural Service Guilds:
- Testing Laboratories:

Present Role of the Department

Andhra Pradesh has become a State of opportunities in the scenario of economic liberalization for establishing major, small scale and cottage industries. In this scenario, the objectives of the Department are:

- To make Andhra Pradesh the foremost industrialized State in the country.
- To provide the right environment for capability building of the industry.

- To create a hassle free environment for attracting both foreign and domestic investment.
- To provide quality infrastructure.
- To facilitate healthy growth of industries.

To sum up the following are the major functions at present scenario in the department of Industries. Since the Commissioner of Industries is the Nodal Agency for investment promotion and industrial development in Andhra Pradesh and would be in a position to assist the entrepreneur/ investors in providing.

- Latest updates on Union & State Govt. policies.
- Information on Investment Opportunities.
- Comprehensive guidance on obtaining clearances/ approvals from Central and State Governments.
- The prescribed forms of Central and State Government for submitting applications for the required clearances/approvals.
- Introduction to other departments of Government.
- Escort services during the course of implementation of the projects.
- Co-ordination through organizing meetings for investors with concerned officials. of other Govt. departments wherever required.
- Match making for joint ventures.

As briefly detailed above the department of Industries, Government of Andhra Pradesh and Amara Raja Batteries are chosen for a comparative study of Human Resource Development and this comparative study will bring out the relative advantages and contributions to employment generation, economic development, utilization of advancing technology benefiting the individual initiators towards entrepreneurship development both on the part of department of Industries at state level and the primary batteries with its head quarters at Tirupati in Andhra Pradesh.

REFERENCES

1. Department Manual, Department of Industries- Developed by Dr.MCRHRDIAP , Hyderabad
2. www.apind.gov.in
3. Brochures of Amararaja Batteries
4. Amara Raja Manual Amara Raja Companies Profile prepared by the Company

6

ANALYSIS OF RESPONSES OF THE SAMPLE RESPONDENTS OF THE DEPARTMENT OF INDUSTRIES, GOVERNMENT OF ANDHRA PRADESH

In accordance with the objectives of the study relevant questionnaires were formulated and administered to a sample of executives and operational level employees both in the Government Sector – Department of Industries Government of Andhra Pradesh and Amara Raja Batteries Pvt. Ltd., of Private Sector. In the following pages we go in for analysis and interpretation based on the responses secured from the personnel of the Department of Industries and selected DICs (District Industries Centres).

The following discussion is related to the opinion and ideas of 10 executives of the Department of Industries, Government of Andhra Pradesh.

The questionnaire administered covered the following aspects:

a) Importance accorded to training

b) Work commitment on the part of the employees

c) The work environment

d) Workers participation in formulating and in achieving goals and objectives of the organisation.

e) Inter-personal relations

f) Prospects towards career development.

g) Work culture

From the Department of Industries, 10 executives were administered a separate questionnaire. The following are the responses obtained from the 10 executives.

Pre-Entry and other training programmes

It was reported by 10 executives that pre-entry training is normal and routine which is also called induction training.

In respect to the induction training/pre-entry training as per the respondents it lasts for 21 days. On some occasions 21 days of induction training is conducted twice, each time lasting for 10 to 11 days. It is in respect to the convenience of the administration and they also feel splitting of pre-entry training into two parts is effective and contributing to the participants.

In regard to the short programmes offered on specific areas the duration ranges from 3- 5 days. It may be mentioned here that the Department of Industries has a separate wing for organizing training programmes for its employees on its own campus.

It is made mandatory on the part of the Department of Industries to provide training to all the employees. Here the term employees comprises administrative, operational and executives on an average as reported by the respondents each employee spends 7.80 days in training.

Medium of Instruction

In respect to medium of instruction in training both on the campus and outside institutions it is usually in English and occasionally using local language Telugu. In respect to the training of the top and middle level executives, the medium of instruction is English. It may be mentioned here that the training programme depends on the comprehension on the part of the participants and also sensing and understanding on the part of the trainer. To make the employees understand Telugu language is used explaining the significance and import of what has been explained in English language.

Board and lodging facilities

It may be mentioned here that on the campus of the training institute both at the State level and at the District level. It was reported that they don't have facilities of board and lodging for the participants. But in the case of employees sent for training other training institutes, the participants are provided with board and lodging facilities on the campus of the training institutes.

Here we may mention that Dr. Marri Channa Reddy Human Resource Development Institute of A.P. (Dr. MCR HRD IAP) is a premier institute located in Hyderabad which organizes more than 300 programmes every year in different areas. On this campus very comfortable board and lodging facilities are provided. Often, the Department of Industries, A.P. and other States in the country sponsor different levels of employees for training at this institute. In this respect it is the State of Andhra Pradesh, Department of Industries which sponsors a considerable number of it's employees for training at this institute. Dr MCR HRD IAP functions as a nodal training institute in the state of Andhra Pradesh.

Since it is a specific and special area with regard to the functions of the department, it was reported that there are internal trainers also in the department who sometimes and often join the designated formal trainers in providing training in specific areas and promote department of small scale and medium scale enterprises in the State.

When the programmes are organised on the campus very often the department invites guest faculty from training institutes in the relevant field. As usual relevant reading material concerning the themes included in the programme is prepared in advance and provided to the participants.

Employees behaviour and commitment

It was reported by 3 out of 10 respondents interviewed that the employees are good in effectively co-operating with the jobs of the department. 6 respondents out of 10 said that the employees' co-operation in the department is contributing to the objectives of the department. One among the 10 respondents simply said that the employees in the department are co-operative with the functions thereof.

Any strikes in the Department

It is quiet interesting to note that the Department of Industries has never indulged in any kind of strike since its inception. It is really interesting to note this fact. Though there were no strikes the employees in a peaceful and positive way brought to the notice of the authorities to consider salary enhancement.

Essential training programmes to be organized to the employees

When the question was asked to the respondents about the essential training programmes that are to be organized, the respondents came up with the following suggestions:

a. Communication skills

b. Inter-personal relations

c. Team Building

d. Working skills relevant to the activity.

e. Awareness programmes in respect to domain of small

& medium scale industries – innovation of new technology.

Employees Participation in Policy Decisions

In any industrial organisation policy formulation and setting of goals and objectives is a primary and ever relevant principle. When 10 of the executive staff in the department were asked whether there is employee participation in department policy formulation and setting up of the objectives, 5 respondents opined they should participate in such critical policy formulation and 4 respondents opined that there was no need for them to participate in such crucial and critical events and 1 respondent remained silent to this question.

Contribution of Training

In respect to the question to the contribution of training imparted to the employees to what extent it really enhances performance and contributes to the goals and objectives of the organisation, one out of 10 executives interviewed remained silent and not responsive whereas, 6 respondents have indicated that the training was rather moderate in contributing knowledge, skills and positive attitudinal change towards the specific objective of action and 3 respondents opined that the effectiveness was substantial.

It may be mentioned here that the department personnel meet once in a month to review the progress of the activities of the department. In this regard it may be mentioned here at the district level District Industries Centres (DICs), the General Manager organizes and conducts a monthly meeting to review the progress of small scale industrial development in the district in its various dimensions.

It is to be mentioned here in this connection that monthly meetings as a regular schedule are conducted at every DIC and the proceedings and resolutions are submitted to the

District Collector of the particular district. The monthly meetings are related to:

a) Inputs

b) Technology

c) Resources and Manpower

d) Personnel problems

Plans of the executives in respect to training programmes to be offered to the employees:

In respect to the question the type of training programmes to be offered to the employees, based on their observations and experience, they suggested to impart training to the employees for their effective performance in the following areas:

a) Provide training on latest trends based on domain knowledge and skills.

b) Interpersonal relations and communication

c) Making employees to work in teams (Team Building).

d) Personality Development, career development and

e) Participative Management.

Individual Employee Questionnaire Analysis:-

In the Department of Industries including DICs there are 890 employees in administration and operational level. Out of this total number, the researcher has taken 10% of the total employees choosing 6 DICs and Administrative office at Hyderabad. A separate structured questionnaire was administered to the 90 respondents and their responses are discussed below:

Table 1
Age of the Respondents

Age	*Below 30*	*31 – 40*	*Above 40*	*Total respondents*	*Total Percentage*
No. of respondents	22	47	21	90	
Percentage	24.44%	52.22%	23.34%	-	100.00

You find different age groups working in the organization are shown in the above table. In respect to the sex of the respondents there are 78 male and 12 female in the sample chosen.

Table 2
Educational Qualifications of the respondents

Educational qualifications	*Post graduates*	*Graduates*	*Total*	*Percentage*
No. of respondents	10	80	90	-
Percentage	31.25%	68.75%	-	100.00

In the area of post graduation we find some of the respondents are of M. Tech. (Masters in Technology) and in the graduate group also majority of the respondents are with B. Tech. (Bachelor of Technology) background. Since, the nature of work in the department is more of technical in nature related to promotion of small scale and medium scale enterprises in different fields. We find a large number of employees with technology back ground.

In respect to the year in which the employee joined the organisation, the responses indicate that the respondents joined the department in different years. In respect to the sample chosen, their joining starts from 1971 and goes up to 2004.

The respondents joined the Department with different designations depending on their qualifications and experience. Some have joined as Asst. Directors, Asst. Managers, Electricians, Accountants, Engineers, Technical Assistants, Junior Officers, Typists, Receptionists, Industrial Promotion Officers, Field Officers and Clerks.

The kind of training programmes underwent by the respondents are

Training Programmes		*No. of Respondents*
a) Leadership skills	-	20
b) Project Management	-	5
c) Seminar on Communication Skills	-	4
d) Revamping Delivery System	-	34
e) Governing for Results	-	17
f) Industrial Safety	-	8
g) Departmental Training	-	2
Total		**90**

Working Environment as perceived by the employees

Working environment is a crucial factor related to and contributing to the Human Resource Development. It reflects the attitude and commitment on the part of the employees. It is a conducive and motivating factor to the employees while they work they enjoy their work because of the encouraging environment and conditions. Work environment consists of the physical infrastructure, facilities and healthy human relations. In the following table the views/ impressions expressed by the respondents are shown.

Table 3
Working Environment Perceived by the Employees

Variables	Extremely encouraging	High facilitating	Quite encouraging	Work is supported by others	Highly motivating	Feel happy work	Not satisfactory	Total	per-centage
Respondents	7	10	13	10	7	31	12	90	—
in %	7.78%	11.11%	14.44%	11.11%	7.78%	34.44%	13.34%	—	100

The following Pie diagram explains the above percentages graphically.

Diagram : 1

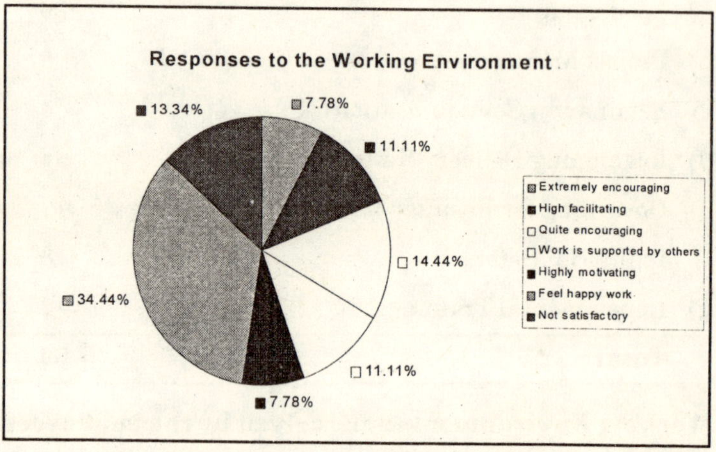

As shown in the table and Pie chart we find diversity of feelings and impressions on the part of the respondents' vis-à-vis the working environment. In general most of the respondents feel happy and appreciative of their working environment. At the same time, we find 12 respondents feeling quite unhappy with the working environment in the organisation.

Career Advancement

In respect to the question based on the respondents job, what kind of training they require for their improvement in the career, the responses are shown in the below table.

Table 4
Career Advancement

Variables	*New Knowledge*	*Advanced Skills*	*Confidence Building*	*Total respondents*	*Per-centage (Total)*
Respondents	63	8	19	90	100
In %	70.00%	8.89%	21.11%	-	100

The following Bar diagram explains the above values graphically at a glance

Diagram : 2

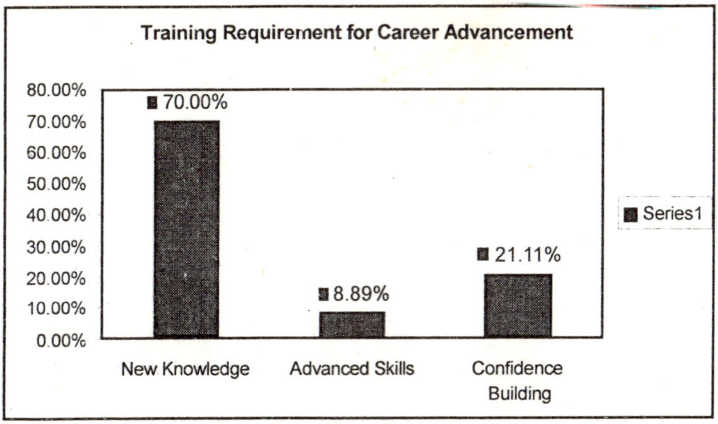

70% of the respondents strongly feel that training programmes are to be organised for them so that they could acquire more relevant knowledge, develop skills, bring about change in attitude, for better understanding of their work and their interaction with the co-workers. 8.89% expressed

they would like to have training programmes focusing on advanced skills in operation.

Further 21.11% of the respondents have expressed that they would like to have training programmes focusing on confidence building. In a sense, it is personal development as well as a sensitivity type of training programme. It may be mentioned here that such programmes are more of practice oriented and enriched by demonstrations. These programmes are related to self-development with confidence building making employees to perform their jobs effectively as expected.

Inter-Personal Relations (IPR)

In any organisation Inter- Personal Relations amongst the subordinates, colleagues and super ordinates is a vital and significant factor in the performance of the employees building up a harmonious work culture which ultimately leads to success and goal achievement of the organisation. Here, we speak of the responses of the respondents as to their feeling and impressions their working with their subordinates, colleagues and their super-ordinates.

Table 5
Responses in respect to working relations with Subordinates

Variables	*Fine*	*Poor/ unhappy*	*Feeling Satisfactory*	*Very Happy*	*No Response*	*Total No. of Respondents*	*Percentage*
Respondents	4	31	39	9	7	90	—
Percentage	4.44%	31.44%	43.33%	10.00%	7.78%	—	100%

The percentages shown in the above table are presented in the following diagram.

Diagram : 3

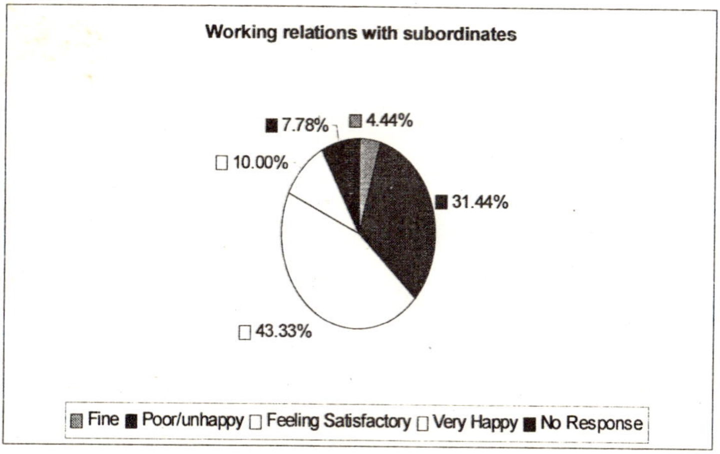

It is interesting to observe diversity of feelings and impressions on the part of the respondents in respect to their working with their subordinates. The majority of the respondents 39 (43.33%) feel happy and their work with their subordinates is satisfactory. This is followed by a contradictory kind of version on the part of 31 (31.44%) respondents who feel that their working relationship with their subordinates is very poor and they feel unhappy working with them.

As a contrast to the above statement 9(10%) respondents have expressed that they are very happy working with their subordinates. This is followed by 4(4.44%) respondents expressing their happiness in working with the subordinates and they use the term 'Fine' for this expression. It is interesting to observe here that 7(7.78%) respondents did not respond to this question. Their non-response also may be construed as their unhappiness or indifference towards their subordinates.

Table 6
Working Relations with Colleagues

Variables	*Good/ Very Happy*	*Not Encouraging*	*No Response*	*Satisfied*	*Happy*	*Total No. of Respondents*	*Percentage*
Respondents	66	17	3	2	2	90	—
Percentage	73.33%	18.89%	3.33%	2.22%	2.22%	—	100%

Diagram : 4

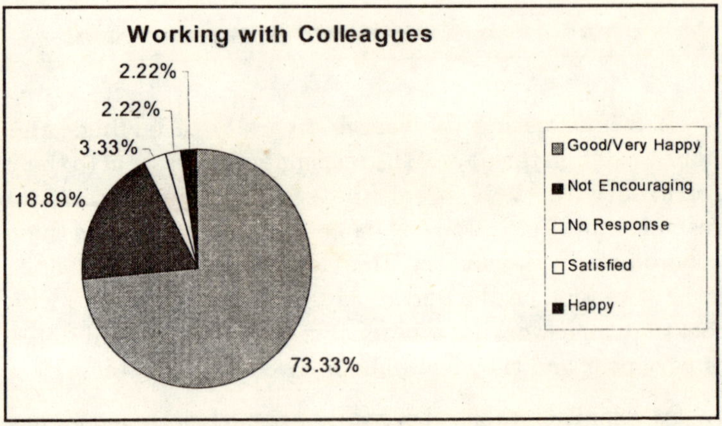

It is interesting to note that 66(73.33%) of the respondents feel that they are very happy in working with their colleagues. And on the other hand 17(18.89%) respondents feel their working with their colleagues is not encouraging which amounts to discard among them. A small number of respondents (2 + 2) feel that they are satisfied and happy working with their colleagues. In this respect also 3(3.33%) respondents did not respond.

Table 7
Responses in respect to working with super-ordinates

Variables	*Good/ Happy*	*Poor / Unhappy*	*Very Happy*	*Not at all Satisfied*	*No Response*	*Total Respondents*	*Percentage*
Respondents	47	29	7	3	4	90	—
Percentage	52.22%	32.22%	7.78%	3.33%	4.44%	—	100%

Diagram : 5

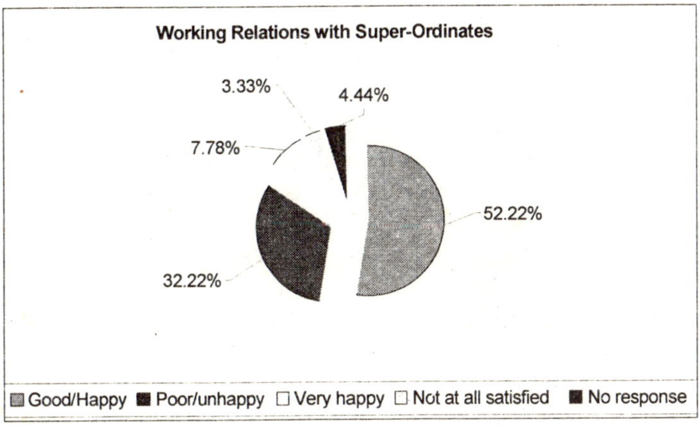

In respect to the respondents' interaction and working with their super-ordinates it is interesting to note that 47(52.22%) respondents have expressed their happiness in working with their super-ordinates. It is followed by a contradictory observation expressed by 29 (32.22%) respondents. They feel unhappy working with super-ordinates and their working relation with them is poor. On the other hand, it is interesting to note that 7 (7.78%) respondents feel contended or very happy working with their super-ordinates. In this respect we find 3(3.33%) respondents indicating that they are totally unhappy in working with their super-ordinates and 4(4.4%) respondents kept silent when this question was posed. It is usually interpreted as negative and unhappy with their superiors.

Based on the above three dimensions of interactions and working, we see diverse responses. The question is whether it is to be attributed to the individual psyche and personality or it is something wanting or defect on the other hand. We come across different perceptions within the same organisation and same kind of personnel with similar kind of activities and responsibilities entrusted to the individual employees whether they are super-ordinates, sub-ordinates or colleagues. In a sense, these responses of the 90 respondents more or less reflect the situation and the working relationship among different categories of personnel in most of the organizations- Public, Private or Government. Here, we have been dealing with a Department of Government who were supposed to work in cohesion translating the purposes and objectives of the department. It may not be out of place to observe that the employees of the department are not working in unison to translate the objectives of the department, it is rather unfortunate. Understanding and co-ordination among various levels of employees in an organisation – top level executives, middle level supervisors and lower level operators is minimal and wanting. And here comes the need for examining such unsatisfactory and painful situations and go in for remedial measures in terms of counselling, training and overall streamlining of work environment and a regular, realistic study of factors that are the cause for this kind of diversity of feelings, impressions and experiences among staff of an organisation.

The satisfactory or unsatisfactory feelings are to be attributed to the real experiences of the employees at different levels or to different personalities of the individual employees. In a word it is either the richness or the short comings on the part of the employees which brings out the diverse experiences.

Suggestions offered by the respondents to improve the working conditions are:

Before we go to the suggestions, it is felt that there is a need to explain some of the concepts used in this context.

1. Work culture stands for harmonious public relations and good communication.
2. Motivational factors stand for encouraging and enthusing, understanding and commitment to work on the part of the employee striving to achieve standard of excellence in his performance.
3. Training stands for enhancing the requisite knowledge vis-à-vis the job that is performed and to be performed, both technical and managerial skills related to the role of the individual and the requisite attitudinal disposition in respect to the job that is to be accomplished by the individual employee.
4. Organisation and employee relationships refer to the kind of relationship and interaction between the employees and the organisation.
5. Conducive Environment is more of a conceptual nature and it is difficult to spell out in concrete and understandable terms as what constitutes the conducive environment.

The suggestions are grouped into above five categories. Here we mention the suggestions under each category.

1. Work culture

- Cooperation between employees is to be created. Interpersonal relations, motivation should be improved.
- Collective responsibility is to be created.
- Everybody should work hard. It means everybody should have a commitment towards ones work.
- Internal meetings should be conducted to resolve the internal conflicts.

- Reduce the duplication of work.
- Shared vision, mutual understanding and coordination is needed.
- Transparency must be there.
- More cooperation and support is needed from the top management and
- Identify the workers' abilities and improve the employee motivation.

2. Motivational factors:

- Qualification based position and responsibilities are entrusted to the employees.
- Job rotation should be there.
- Benefits like promotion and incentives are provided by the company.
- Efficiency should be encouraged.
- The organisation should take always innovative and challenging projects.
- Transportation facilities to be provided to all Industrial Promotion Officers in well developed industrial area and
- Empower Industrial Promotion Officers in the District Industrial Centres.

3. Training:

- Training should be conducted for every two months so that our strengths and weaknesses are identified.
- Training should be given in latest trends (in domain area) to meet the requirements of competition.
- Mindset to be changed.
- Suggestions from field and executive staff should be given importance.
- Technical training to maintain files in a systematic way through Computers and
- Personality Development training to be conducted periodically for all the employees.

4. Organisation & Employee Relationship:

- Need to appoint more Industrial Promotion Officers.
- Decentralization of power.
- Logical approach and conclusion.
- Department should concentrate more on industrialization.

5. Conducive Environment:

- An informal climate to be created.
- Provide minimum infrastructure facilities to all the employees.

It is rather essential to show the number of respondents who have made a particular suggestion and these details are shown in the table that follows the list of suggestions

Table 8
Suggestions offered by employees to improve work conditions

Variables	*Work Culture*	*Moti-vational Factors*	*Training*	*Org. & Employee Relation*	*Conducive Environ-ment*	*No Response*	*Total*	*Percentage*
No. of Respondents	15	15	14	10	6	30	90	
Percentage	16.67%	16.67%	15.56%	11.11%	6.67%	44.50%		100

Diagram : 6

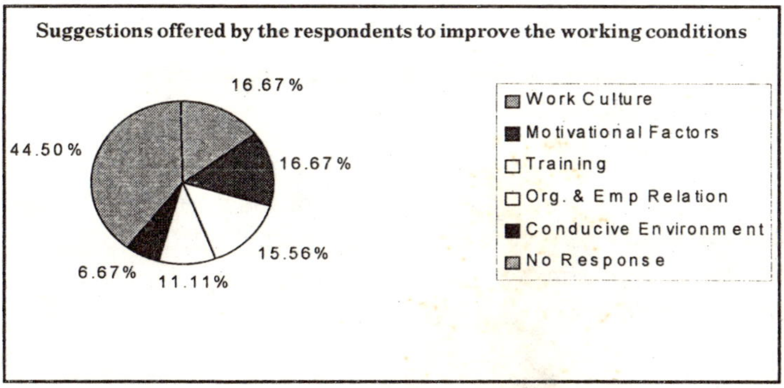

As shown in the table and Diagram above 15(16.67%) respondents expressed the view that work culture is to be created strengthened and amplified so that the work of the organisation runs smoothly. Some 15(16.67%) respondents in this respect have indicated the need for motivation to do the present job effectively and to move on positively to higher position of the responsibility. On the other hand, 14 (15.56%) respondents feel that training in the relevant fields is a motivating factor to improve the working conditions in the organisation. In regard to the employees' identity and relationship with the organisation 10 (11.11%) respondents opined the nature and degree of relationship with the employees and the organisation would improve the working conditions. When we speak of conducive environment, it is more of a subjective factor depending on the understanding on the part of the respondents.

It may not be out of place here to mention what is conducive situation or environment for one may not hold good for another. In regard to what you call conducive environment you have different perceptions. In respect to this item, 6 (6.67%) respondents have indicated the need for a conducive environment for effective working. It is interesting to note that 30 (44.50%) respondents out of 90 did not respond to this question. It is rather difficult to interpret their non-response in respect to this question. Often we come across employees in organisations who are non-committal, they seldom vote for a or b and remain silent. There are ideological, personal reasons and also lack of confidence and anticipated fear of consequences.

When the respondents were asked whether they know the objectives of the organisation, 81 of them indicated that they know and while the remaining kept silent. This silence may mean that these respondents were rather better off or not interested to express their opinions.

In respect to the question whether the employees have any prospects for their career development in the organisation the following are the responses:

When we look at the responses in respect of their career advancement in the organization majority of the respondents (43) conveyed that they don't have any career advancement in the organization. And at the same time there is no response from 18 employees on this aspect and 9 employees responded that there are no career prospects at all in the organization. This factor demotivates the employees which hampers the work in the organization.

Having analysed the various aspects of HRD in the industries department, Government of Andhra Pradesh now let us move to analyse the situation in Private Sector unit - Amara Raja Batteries Limited.

7

ANALYSIS OF RESPONSES OF THE SAMPLE RESPONDENTS OF THE AMARA RAJA BATTERIES PRIVATE LIMITED

In this Chapter we look into the responses obtained from Amara Raja Batteries, the sample unit from private sector. The profile of this organisation is clearly discussed in Chapter IV. As in the case of Department of Industries two layers of staff, executives and a combined group of administrative and operational personnel were chosen. In respect to the executive staff 10 were chosen randomly and in the case of administrative and operational personnel 10% of the total population was selected. Separate structured questionnaires were administered to both the selected groups. We will now look into the responses obtained from the executive (10) staff.

In respect of pre-entry training and other programmes

The first question administered to the executives relates to whether there is pre-entry training after the selection of the candidates to the designated posts. All the ten respondents conveyed that there is pre-entry training for all selected personnel.

In respect to the duration of the pre-entry training programme majority of the officers conveyed that it varies from 3–5 days and in some cases the duration varies in between 6-10 days.

In respect of technical training focusing on skill and operational techniques, the training programmes were conducted for 30 days. As one could see it is practice oriented where the training focuses on each individual participant helping him gain practical and operational knowledge.

It may be mentioned here that Amara Raja Batteries has its own induction training centre. The kind of products they manufacture and the vast geographical area they cover for marketing demands ISO-standards. So the organisation is very particular in training each individual to attain standard of excellence, knowledge and operational skills related to products they manufacture. One could see the importance that is given to training of the personnel and all categories of employees are trained.

In Amara Raja Batteries there is no fixed schedule of training programmes, but the training offered to the employees is need based. In this respect one employee depending on the department or section where he works may be trained in a year from 1 to 5 times and the organisation periodically goes in for assessing the training needs on the part of the employees when new technology in manufacturing is adopted by the company. Training is need and demand based. At the same time, some of the employees who are in the marginal areas, a kind of support personnel may not have any training even for 3 or 4 years.

Medium of Instruction

Since the company is located in Andhra Pradesh near Tirupati predominantly a Telugu speaking area normally Telugu is medium of instruction in the training programme.

But in view of the trickle technical nature of training where in largely the material is published in English language, whether they are books or pamphlets, the resident trainers and often visiting/ guest faculty normally use English in their lectures and their communication with the participants. But in general, both English & Telugu are used in the class room. Usually, the notes given and reading material provided to the participants is in English language only.

Board & Lodging facilities

Amara Raja Batteries has vast and excellent infrastructure to provide board and lodging facilities for the out station participants.

Behaviour of the Employees and their commitment

The 10 executive respondents operating at the apex level opined that the conduct and behaviour of the employees numbering 1060 are good and acceptable.

Any strikes in the organisation

As per the version of the respondents there has not been any strike by the employees since it's inception of the organisation.

Since it is product-manufacturing organisation where quality and service are of primary importance, the organisation has built in a system of continuous feedback to the employees, so that they may no where they have failed in keeping the expected standards in making things. This continuous assessment and feedback is to be considered as an important informal training which is imparted to the employees.

The respondents suggested that the following programmes may be organized for their employees:

Suggested Training Programmes to be organized to the employees:

1. Latest trends in batteries manufacturing technology.
2. Career development programmes.
3. Team Building.
4. Interpersonal relations and communication.

Employee participation in policy decision making

In respect to middle level and lower level employees' participating in policy decisions, the response from the executive respondents is 'No' which means the policy formulation question does not go beyond the executive staff. It is understood that it is the management and occasionally inviting top level executives involvement in policy decisions and policy formulations.

Contribution of Training

From the respondents view point the contribution of training to the organization is substantial in terms of products, rendering of product related service in client system.

To the question of periodicity of the meetings conducted it is said meetings are held fortnightly and some times monthly.

The meetings are held in the following areas to make the employees to participate:

a) Production
b) Technology
c) Marketing and
d) Personnel problems.

Individual Employees Questionnaire Analysis:-

In this part we focus on employees(Administrative

and Operational) in the organisation. The total number, both administrative and operational, is 1060. Out of this 10% was selected using the random sample method. Though as per the 10% sample, it comes to 106 but the researcher has made it to 110 for statistical use. As mentioned in the case of executive staff, a separate questionnaire was administered to all the 110 respondents and their responses were discussed below:

Table 9
Age of the respondents

Age	*Below 30*	*31 – 40*	*Above 40*	*Total Age*	*Total Percentage*
No. of respondents	57	46	7	110	
Percentage	51.82%	41.82%	6.36%		100%

The spread of different age groups working in the organisation are shown in the above table. Among them majority (57) of the employees in the organization, is below 30, followed by below 40 age group numbering 46(41.82%) employees. When we speak of the age of the employees since, the business in this organization is mostly technology oriented, we find a large number of employees with academic and technology background.

In respect to the sex of the respondents, there are 80 male and 30 female. This proportion of male and female in the organisation is encouraging where we find considerable number of female employees with technical academic qualifications. It may be mentioned here in most of the industrial organisations in India we don't find this proportion of female male ratio.

Table 10
Educational Qualifications of the Respondents

Educational Qualifica-tions	*Post Graduates*	*Graduates*	*Inter/ITI*	*Total No. of respondents*	*Total Percentage*
No. of respondents	22	76	12	110	-
Percentage	20.00%	69.09%	10.91%	-	100

The above table shows the educational background of the sample of employees.

The sample of employees under discussion joined the company in various years beginning 1985 and upto 2004. This kind of periodic recruitment as reported depends on two factors. First the retirement of personnel and some leaving the organisation may be for better opportunities elsewhere. Secondly, wherever new technology is introduced and with expansion and diversification of activities the company goes in for selection of new employees. Majority of sample respondents have been recruited after 1990s with expansion and diversification of activity and after adoption of new technology.

The employees under discussion have joined this company as indicated below:

Some have joined as Quality Control Engineers, Asst. Managers, Electricians, Mechanical employees, Accountants, Engineers, Technical Assistants, Sr. Analysts, Jr. Analysts, Supervisors, Management Trainees, Junior Officers, Typists, Receptionists.

The following training programmes were conducted in the organization.

Training Programmes		*Number*
1. Leadership skills	-	13
2. Motivation	-	21
3. Communication skills	-	14
4. Technological training	-	20
5. Automation	-	09
6. Quality Management Services	-	03
7. Awareness on ISO 9001 – 2000	-	07
8. Quality control	-	01
9. No response	-	22
Total	:	110

Out of total respondents chosen for the study 22 candidates have not responded to this question. May be they would not have been nominated for any training or they could not avail the training due to personal reasons. We come across some cases wherein some senior, middle aged or aged employees even if they are nominated for training, they feel reluctant to attend the training emphasizing that they are so experienced.

Table 11
Working environment as perceived by the respondents

Variables	*Extremely encouraging*	*Highly facilitating*	*Quiet encouraging*	*Work is supported by others*	*Highly motivating*	*Feel happy working*	*Total no. of respondents*	*Total percentage*
No. of respondents	21	19	32	13	9	16	110	
Percentage	19.09%	17.27%	29.09%	11.82%	8.18%	14.55%	—	100%

The percentages in the above table are reflected in the diagram given below.

Diagram : 7

Working Environment

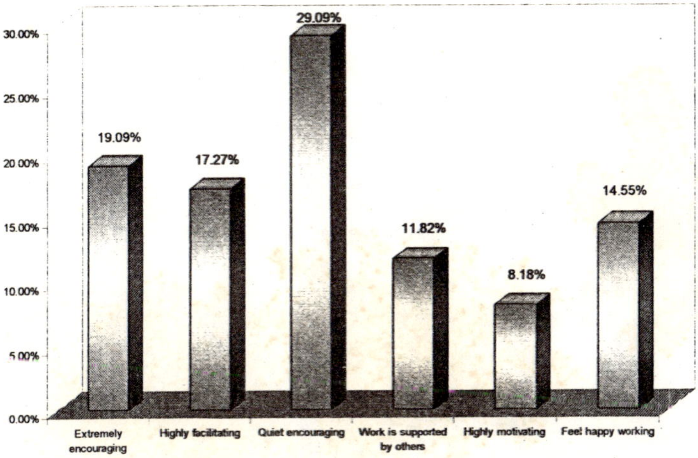

The table 11 shows overall environment is highly encouraging. No respondent has indicated anything negative and wanting in the working environment. In brief, the working environment is conducive, stimulating and pleasant. One could see the feeling on the part of the respondents in respect to the working environment conditioning significantly as a HRD factor. To have such a positive feeling on the part of the entire group is really appreciable and rare in some of the cases. One may go into the details as to the physical, material and human constituents creating such a satisfactory and conducive environment making employees work with pleasure. This kind of a situation not only satisfies the worker, but overall productivity and a positive image on the part of the organization.

Table 12

Kinds of Training needed as expressed for upward movement of employees

Variables	*New knowledge*	*Advanced skills*	*Confidence building*	*New Knowledge advanced skills*	*Total No. of respondents*	*Total Per-centage*
No. of respondents	30	47	17	16	110	—
Percentage	27.27%	42.73%	15.45%	14.55%	—	100

Diagram : 8

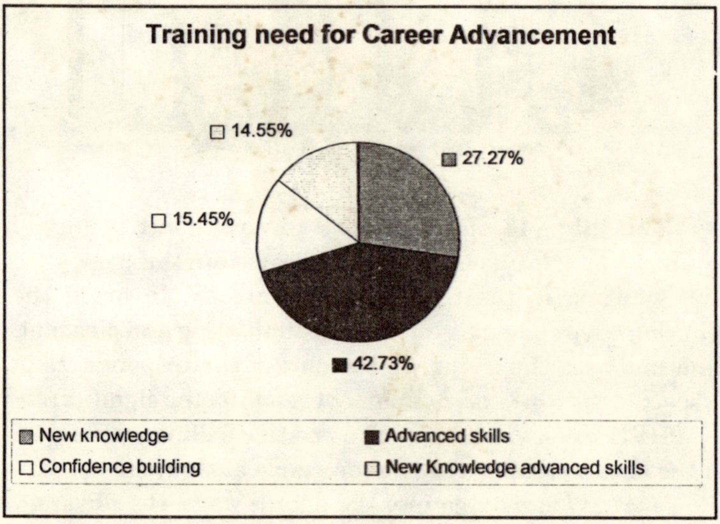

It is really appreciable to note that the respondents are aware the kind of knowledge and skills required for their upward movement in their career, whether in the same parent organisation or elsewhere when the opportunity arise. This knowledge as to the kind of training required is positive and encouraging on the part of the respondents that is in simple terms, the respondents are career growth oriented and knowledgeable. Since, they know the requirements which would facilitate moving forward in their career, it is not out of place to mention that we have a healthy and progressive human element among the respondents in the organisation.

As shown in the table 12 and diagram (9) majority of the respondents (47) have indicated that they require training in advanced skills related to the prospective jobs in the same type of the present job. On the other hand, 30 respondents have said that they need advanced knowledge in the present field where they are engaged. It is interesting to note that 17 respondents require training which would facilitate confidence building among their colleagues, co-workers and their super-ordinates. This kind of a suggestion on the part of these respondents is the outcome of their experience.

But, in case of other 16 respondents, they expressed that they need training both in the areas of new knowledge and advanced skills related to the field of work they are presently engaged in. It may be observed here not as an exaggeration, the sample of participants in the organisation might be looking for opportunities and means which would facilitate their advancement in their career. It is a positive indication of enlightened human resources.

Table 13

Inter-Personal Relations (IPR) with Subordinates

Variables	*Fine*	*Poor / unhappy*	*Feel happy / satisfactory*	*Very happy*	*Co-operative respondents*	*No. of respondents*	*Total no. of*	*Total percentage*
No. of respondents	14	10	27	8	1	50	110	—
Percentage	12.73%	9.09%	24.55%	7.27%	0.91%	45.45%	—	100

Diagram : 9

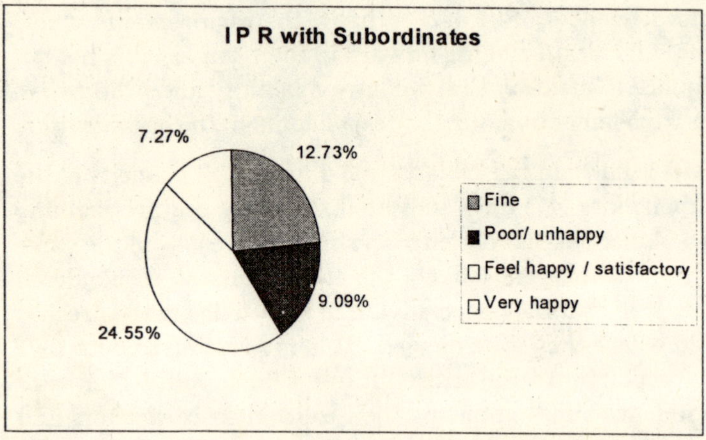

In respect to Inter-Personal Relations (IPR) with reference to the sample respondents, the overall atmosphere appears to be unsatisfactory. This unsatisfactory relationship is in respect to subordinates. Normally, the super-ordinates very rarely appreciate and speak in positive terms in their relationships with their subordinates. Not that the superior officials do not appreciate the working and contribution of their subordinates in the organisation. Sometimes, it may be a traditional kind of tendency or a stereo type of thing where super-ordinates seldom or rarely appreciate the work of their subordinates. It may be really based on facts of performance or a tendency often to say the work of the subordinates is not satisfactory sometimes thinking and imagining this kind of opinion will really motivate the subordinates towards hard work and improvement in their jobs.

As we have shown in the table 13 and diagram 10 where in 27 (24.55%) respondents have indicated that they feel happy and satisfied with the performance of their subordinates while 14(12.73%) respondents have opined that the work of the subordinates is fine. On the other hand, 10 of the respondents have expressed that the performance of the subordinates is poor and they feel unhappy about their work. On the other extreme a small number of respondents 8 (7.27%) feel happy about the work of the subordinates.

It is to be noted here that nearly 50 (45.45%) respondents did not respond to this question which may be interpreted as their dissatisfaction with the work contributed by their subordinates. As mentioned above, non-response from such a large number of respondents is to be construed in negative terms.

The present study is not an isolated one looking into the working relationship between colleagues, super-ordinates and subordinates. One may venture to say this kind of a situation, experience, opinions and images are common in many of the organisations. There may be a few organisations where there is exceptional understanding, co-ordination and harmonious working relationship among colleagues, subordinates and super-ordinates.

Table 14
Inter-Personal Relations with colleagues

Variables	*Good/ Very happy*	*Satisfied*	*Not encouraging*	*Happy*	*Very Poor*	*No. of respond-ents*	*Total no. of respond-ents*	*Total per-centage*
No. of respondents	72	13	3	7	2	13	110	—
Percentage	65.65%	11.82%	2.73%	6.36%	1.82%	11.82%	—	100

Diagram : 10

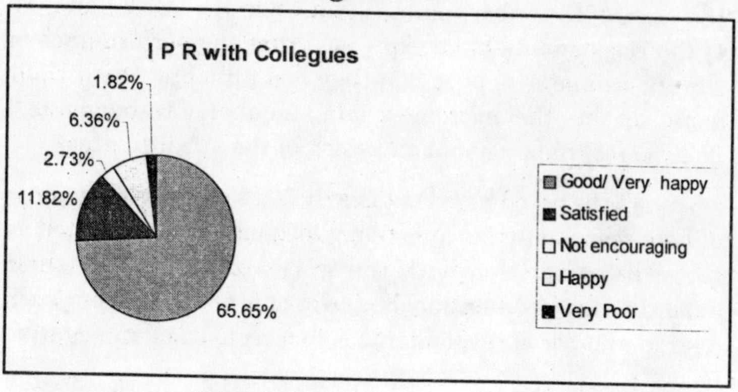

In respect to the kind of understanding and working relationship among the colleagues of the same level, majority of respondents 72 (65.65%)] have expressed that their relationship with their colleagues is good and they feel happy in working with them. It is a good and positive sign of coordination among the colleagues. There may be exceptions to the generality of this kind of feeling and impression related to working with the colleagues.

One may not find common and stereotype of relationships among the colleagues in work situation. There are and there may be different perceptions and experiences. For example, in the present case 13 (11.82%) have expressed that they are satisfied working with their colleagues and 7 (6.36%) respondents have indicated that they feel happy working with their colleagues. In contrast to this, just a small number of (3+2) have expressed that working with colleagues is not encouraging and they don't feel happy.

It is as mentioned elsewhere in this analysis, 13 (11.82%) respondents did not answer this particular question. This non-response is primarily to be stated as dissatisfaction and unhappiness working with the colleagues. Though there was enough time and freedom on the part of the respondents who were administered a structured questionnaire in the present study they had an opportunity to indicate their feelings, impressions and judgments whatsoever but they did not respond. It is not simply going beyond the premises of this analysis, but the non-response of 13 respondents is indicative of their dissatisfaction or unhappiness vis-à-vis working with their colleagues.

Table 15

Inter-Personal Relations with Super-ordinates

Variables	*Good/ Very happy*	*Not at all Satisfied*	*Encouraging/ Co-operative*	*Poor*	*Very happy respondents*	*No response centage*	*Total no. of*	*Total per-*
No. of respondents	23	19	9	6	5	48	110	—
Percentage	20.91%	17.27%	8.18%	5.45%	4.55%	43.64%	—	100%

Diagram : 11

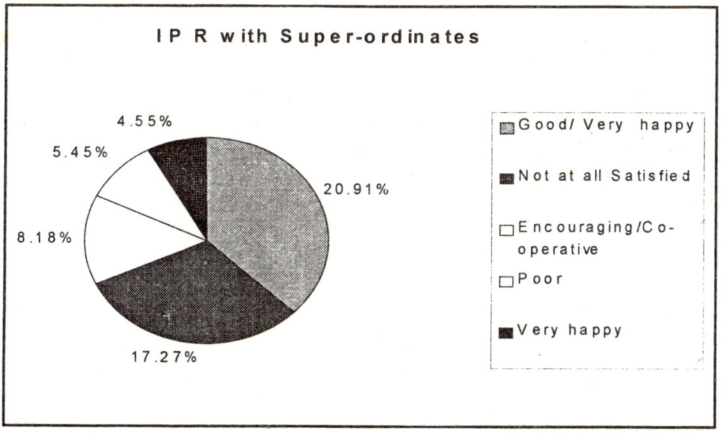

Normally, when it comes to opinion and assessment of subordinate staff in respect to super-ordinate staff which in a broad sense constitutes the managerial umbrella. You will come across a mixed kind of reaction both positive and negative. In respect to views and impressions and experiences of the subordinates and the manner the super-ordinates treat, encourage and motivate their subordinates is rather variegated. In the present context, while 23 (20.91%) of the respondents have indicated that they are happy and appreciative of working with the super-ordinates a contrary opinion was expressed by another 19 (17.27%) respondents that they are not at all satisfied working with the super-ordinates. 9 (8.18%) respondents have indicated that their working with super-ordinates is encouraging and very co-operative. More or less, in a similar way 5 (4.55%) respondents have expressed their unhappiness working with the super-ordinates. Contrary to this impression 6 (5.45%) respondents have indicated that their relationship with their super-ordinates is poor. It is a negative indication.

It is really interesting to note 48 (43.64%) respondents did not answer this question, which may be interpreted as mentioned elsewhere unhappiness working under their superior officers.

It is not a question of repetition, but restatement that really you may have cordial appreciative and happy relationship amongst all layers of employees in a given organisation. This relates to human values, expectations, life experiences of diverse nature. It is rather difficult to arrive at and establish a stereo type of mechanical system of operation and conducting a business in any field.

Suggestions offered by the respondents to improve the working conditions

Table 16

Variables	*Work Culture*	*Motivation factors*	*Training*	*Organisation of employee relationships*	*Conducive environment*	*No respondents*	*Total No. of Response*	*Total Percentage*
No. of respondents	11	3	32	2	4	59	110	—
Percentage	10.00%	2.73%	29.09%	0.91%	3.64%	53.64%	—	100%

Diagram : 12

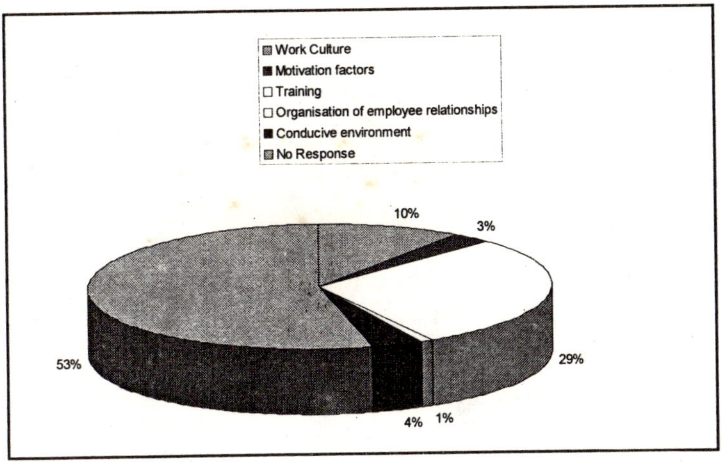

It is very interesting to note here that 59(53.64%) respondents out of 110 did not respond in respect to the question whether they offer any suggestions to improve the working conditions in the organisation. It is rather difficult to interpret their non-response. Often we come across employees in organisations who are non-committal, they seldom think of the organisation. But, we may not take and apply the same phenomena in this context because their non-response may be taken as that either they did not understand properly the question itself or they would lack spontaneous ideas to respond.

As we have shown in the table 16 above 11(10%) of respondents pointed out that they need work culture in the organisation to improve the working conditions so that in turn it contributes to enthuse individuals. So the work of the organisation runs smoothly. Very less 3(2.73%) respondents bother about motivational factors. When it comes to conducive environment 4(3.64%) expressed that management should create conducive environment. In respect of training a large number i.e. 32(29.09%) respondents responded that training contributes a lot to enthuse the individual. At the same time, training gives scope for career advancement in the organisations. It also motivates the individuals to a great deal.

It may be mentioned here that the respondents have come out with a number of suggestions for the sake of analysis. The suggestions made by the respondents are grouped into the following generic frame.

a) Work culture b) Motivational factors c) Training d) Organisation & Employee Relations e) Conducive environment

The above concepts have been defined in earlier chapters

1. Work culture:

- Cooperation between employees is to be created. Interpersonal relations, motivation should be improved.
- Commitment and ownership to be created.
- Internal meetings should be conducted to resolve the internal conflicts.
- Shared vision, mutual understanding and coordination is needed.
- Identify the workers' abilities and improve the employee motivation

2. Motivational factors:

- Qualification based position and responsibilities are entrusted to the employees.
- Job rotation should be there.
- Benefits like promotion and incentives are provided by the company.

- Efficiency should be encouraged.
- The organisation should take always innovative and challenging projects.

3. **Training:**

- Training should be conducted for every two months so that our strengths and weaknesses are identified.
- Training should be given in latest trends (in domain area) to meet the requirements of competition.
- Mindset to be changed.
- Technical training to maintain files in a systematic way through Computers and
- Personality Development training to be conducted periodically for all the employees.

4. **Organisation & Employee Relationship**

- Decentralization of power.
- Logical approach and conclusion.

5. **Conducive Environment:**

- An informal climate to be created.
- Provide minimum infrastructure facilities to all the employees.

The suggestions offered by the respondents are of generic in nature. One has to go into the substance, elements and parameters of every suggestion made by the respondents. On just looking at them they sound vague. One may have to go deeper in respect to the specific ideas, content and its implications in respect of each suggestion made by the respondents. But the suggestions are clear in general and usual sense, however, they are to be analysed and arrived at concrete implementable measures in order to use them to make the working conditions clearly transparent and easily affordable. It's something usual that often we come across such type of good, positive, unprejudiced suggestions, but one has to go deeper and spell out the relevant elements in the suggestion that are offerable and translated into action.

In respect to the question whether the sample respondents have any knowledge of the aims and objectives of the organisation where they are employed. In this context, rarely all the employees in an organisation know the vision and objectives of the particular organisation. Many of them have vague ideas about the organisations.

It is really encouraging to find that 103 out of 110 respondents i.e. over 90% have indicated that they know the aims and objectives of the organisation where they work. This kind of a statement that they have the total knowledge cannot be taken on its face value. It is not just a comment, but usually people say they know. But one has to look into the details and the depth of knowledge they possess vis-à-vis, the organisation where they work. In some of these areas both vagueness and clarity of concepts, ideas etc. happen. In some cases you may be provided with a clear cut analysis or details of a project, its intentions and implications related to a particular segment of the population.

In respect to the question whether the employees have any prospectus they find for their career development in the organisation the following are responses:

When we look at the responses 20 employees said there is no progress or career advancement in the organization. 20 employees did not respond. In one way they expressed dissatisfaction by not responding.

28 employees responded in a positive way. This is a good sign of satisfaction on the part of the employees. The other remaining respondents also responded in a positive way. This

is a very good sign of motivation towards their work in the organization.

Having analysed the HRD aspects in Industries Department of Government of Andhra Pradesh and AmaraRaja Batteries independently now let us analyse both the sectors in a comparative perspective.

8

COMPARATIVE ANALYSIS OF THE DEPARTMENT OF INDUSTRIES AND AMARA RAJA BATTERIES

Human Resource Development is recognized as a humane intellectual and, motivational input for the advancement of the individual in his career and his maximal contribution to the organisation for its growth and development. One could see the application of essential elements of HRD in a two faced sense helps the individual and an organisation in their aspirations and development. Though HRD has been recognized during the recent past as a necessary input in organisations, it is being put into practice in varied degrees often out of not realizing the importance of HRD as a factor contributing to success. The reasons may be financial, sometimes failing to understand the maximal substantial contribution of HRD to the growth and development of the organization. The importance accorded to HRD in organisations varies as varying climatic and weather conditions over the globe. We don't find uniformity and higher degree of intensity in the practice of HRD principles. Earlier and lately it is being recognized as one of the indispensable criteria for the growth of the organization and the individual employee.

The present study focuses on two institutions. One is Department of Industries, Government of Andhra Pradesh and another is a private sector organization. We see at the outset two significant objectives concerning the two organisations taken for study in respect to the place of HRD in these organisations. The Department of Industries is a non- profit oriented, service and promotional agency helping individual entrepreneurs, groups and co-operative institutions. This department helps and provides certain basic facilities such as technical know how, selection of products and requisite machinery, the kind of infrastructure for a particular industry and often guiding the entrepreneurs in marketing their products and encouraging them to make use of available resources. In a word, it is a service organisation guided by the principle of working towards the welfare of the people. The only objective of this organisation is helping the people and self-employed making use of the natural local resources for industrial products and there is no question of monetary profit making in respect to this development in question and all other governmental departments.

When it comes to Amara Raja Batteries, it is an organisation which is primarily profit oriented. Sometimes there may be a sense of service associated with such organisation.

As mentioned earlier, the elements or factors of HRD adopted or put into practice in any organisation vary. One may think of the cost of investment and the increased benefits thereof. For example, one of the basic elements of HRD is providing training to the employees. Organising training means financial investment and expenditure. Even in respect to creating a conducive, harmonious working environment may appear non-monetary, but creating and sustaining such an atmosphere of work also costs money. Therefore, the organisations do not simply and blindly go in for full fledged and wholesome compliment of HRD in organisations. Further, paying attention to HRD also depends on the knowledge of management, feedback from the employees, strikes and sometimes misbehaviour on the part of the workers, dictatorial and authoritative managerial styles, unattainable targets imposed on the employees, lack of understanding between management and senior administrative officers and not seriously considering the day today events and the dynamics that takes place in the organisation. That is they fail to keep a watch over the functioning of the system and fail to identify the shortcomings and the missing links in the operation of the system in the organisations.

Now, let us have a look into the Department of Industries and Amara Raja Batteries for a comparative perspective related to the domain of the Human Resource Development. The following aspects of HRD will be discussed and contrasted in respect to the above two organisations.

From the Responses of Executives

1. Training

    a. Induction training

    b. Duration of the training programme

    c. Internal training

    d. Categories of personnel are trained

    e. Number of programmes an employee undergo in a year

    f. Medium of instruction

    g. Boarding and Lodging facilities

    h. Internal & guest faculty

    i. Providing reading material

2. Behaviour and commitment of the employees in general

3. Participation of employees in decision making
   a. Products
   b. Diversification of activities
   c. Expansion of the organisation
4. Contribution of Training
   a. Substantial
   b. Moderate
   c. Rather minimal
5. Future plans of training to the employees
   From The Responses of Individual (Employees)
6. Working Environment
   a. Extremely encouraging
   b. Highly facilitating
   c. Quite encouraging
   d. Work is supported by others
   e. Highly motivating
   f. Feel happy
   g. Not satisfactory
7. Career Advancement
   a. New/advanced knowledge
   b. Advanced skills
   c. Confidence building
8. Inter-Personal Relations
   a) Subordinates
   b) Colleagues

c) Super-ordinates

9. Suggestions to improve work conditions offered by the employees

   a. Work culture

   b. Training

   c. Motivational factors

   d. Conducive environment

   e. Organisation & Employee Relationships

10. Scope for career advancement

In the present compare and contrast study, we may begin with training component in respect of the higher level administrative staff in the Department of Industries and Amara Raja Batteries. In both the cases as detailed in Chapter 6 and 7, training of the personnel is one of the primary policies of the organisations. In case of Amara Raja Batteries, they have their own facilities within the campus of the organisation. But in the case of Department of Industries, the employees from top to bottom are sent to training centres depending on the nature of the work on the part of the employees. Often the programmes they attend to relate to small scale industrial promotion. But in the case of Amara Raja Batteries the training is more detailed to skill development, so that the products they make have to meet International standards since it is a question of marketing the products to earn profits and stand international competition.

1. **Training**

Employees of both the organisations have pre-entry training/induction training. In the case of Department of Industries the duration of induction training is for 21 days, but in the case of Amara Raja Batteries, the similar training is rather short and lasting 3 – 5 days. In the case of Amara Raja Batteries, the focus of the training is more practice oriented, at this stage new entry employees are exposed to the kind of work they would be doing and the way in which the working system in the organisation is planned and executed.

When we look at induction training in the case of Department of Industries, though it is useful it is rather a stereotype of general training. There will be several inputs in the programme which matter in the course of their service in the department. It is a general exposure type of training, not focusing on any particular aspect of the job to be carried out by the newly inducted members.

It is gathered that Amara Raja Batteries spends per annum Rs.80 lakhs to 1 crore towards organizing training programmes and providing facilities to it's employees. On the other hand the Department of Industries allocates 1-2.5% of budgetary allocation to training and other facilities of it's employees.

2. Behaviour & Commitment on the Part of the Employees

It is interesting to note in general the behaviour and commitment on the part of the employees in both the organisations under the study is viewed as good and appreciable. But there is one exception in the case of Amara Raja Batteries. The sense of 'we' and 'our' products is very dominant. It may be pointed out here that 'we' factor is rather rare in the case of the Department of Industries. The onus in respect to the products and quality, thereof rests on the individuals and groups in the Amara Raja Batteries whereas this kind of individual or collective responsibility is found to be poor in the Department of Industries. The tendency that emerges from the Department of Industries is to find fault with others amounting to "I am O.k., You are not O.k.". As it has been pointed out earlier Amara Raja Batteries is a commercial organisation and it's ethos and nature of working is different from that of Government Departments in general and the Department of Industries in particular. Employees as mentioned above individually and team wise are answerable to the management. Here, the performance is measurable, quantifiable and given a grade, whereas in the case of Department of Industries there is no place for such system.

The accountability and responsibility is specific in Amara Raja Batteries whereas it is fluid and vague in the Department of Industries. Another essential factor of difference is decentralization and delegation of decision making authority. In the case of Amara Raja Batteries, small teams are constituted numbering 3 to 4. These teams are with planning choice of material, technology, the duration within which the targeted products are to be produced. This team works as a unit without often moving upto the management and seeking their advice and guidance. Though the work is carried on with small teams with delegated authority they work within the policy and framework of the organisation. It is observed that the teams work independently and reach the targets very effectively and efficiently.

But in respect of the Department of Industries you have a long chain of authority and hierarchical system. Delegation to the middle and lower staff is rare. Decisions and targets if any come from the above. The hierarchy is such the decision making power mostly rests with the top executive or administrator. The department assists in promoting, guiding and rendering technical advice towards promotion of enterprises only but they are not the industrialists, nor a company working for profit making endeavour.

3. Participation Of Employees In Decision Making

In this context, it may be pointed out that involvement of

the employees except top executives in decision making by management/higher authority is almost nil in both the organisations under study.

4. Contribution of Training

Contribution of training towards efficacious performance on the part of the employees. Training as an input, the question here is to what extent it has contributed or enhanced effective and credit worthy performance on the part of the employees. When we look at the responses both from Department of Industries and Amara Raja Batteries, we don't find much of a difference in their assessment or evaluation of contribution of training towards effective and enhanced performance on the part of employees in both the organisations.

In the case of Amara Raja Batteries 10 executives (100%) have expressed that the training has contributed substantially towards the objectives of the organisation. But in the Department of Industries, 3 (30%) respondents have indicated that training has contributed substantially whereas 6 (60%) have said that training contribution was moderate. One respondent (10%) kept silent and did not respond to this question. It should be construed either as indifference or training as an input has not brought in any change in case of this respondent.

5. Proposed or anticipated training programmes and their contribution to the objectives of the organisation

It is interesting to take note of the knowledge and understanding of the import on the part of the respondents (executives) the expected contribution from the training programmes that have been suggested to be organised in the future. Here, it is not simply repeating a statement, but it is really appreciable that the respondents have realized the importance of the training programmes and their contribution which would enhance the work efficiency on the part of the employees. This is indicative of knowledge in a sense premonition vis-à-vis the importance of relevant training programmes that would encourage, enlighten and prepare the employees for their increased and recognizable contribution to the job that they are expected to perform. In a simple sense training has been recognized by both Amara Raja Batteries and Department of Industries as indispensable input in preparing the employee knowledge wise, skill wise and attitudinal wise vis-à-vis their role in the organisation. The training programmes indicated by the two organisations which they believe would enhance substantially the growth and development of the organisation.

Though, the kind of training programmes suggested by both the organisations mentioned elsewhere in the analysis it may be repeated here;

We list out the training programmes suggested by the Department of Industries and Amara Raja Batteries.

	Department of Industries	*Amara Raja Batteries*
1.	Communication Skills Inter-personal relations	Latest trends in batteries manufacturing technology
2.	Team building	Career development programmes
3.	Working skills relevant to the activity	Team building
4.	Awareness programmes in respect to the domain of small/medium industries - Innovation of new technology	Inter-personal relations and communication

6. How the employees perceive the working environment in both the organisations

In respect to the 90 respondents of the Department of Industries and 110 respondents of the Amara Raja Batteries, the following were the perspectives indicated:

Department of Industries		*Amara Raja Batteries*	
1. Extremely encouraging	08	1. Extremely encouraging	- 21
2. High facilitating	- 10	2. Highly facilitating	- 19
3. Work is supported by others	- 10	3. Work is supported by others	- 13
4. Highly motivating	- 7	4. Highly motivating	- 9
5. Feel happy working	- 31	5. Feel happy working	- 16
6. Quiet encouraging	- 13	6. Quiet encouraging	- 32
7. Not satisfactory	- 11	7. Not satisfactory	- Nil

As we could see from the above two columns in respect to two organisations under study, one could see that there is no indication or any expression of un-satisfaction in Amara Raja Batteries. But at the same time, in respect to the Department of Industries 11 respondents have said the working environment is not satisfactory.

Even if a small number feels not satisfying with the working environment sometimes it will have contageous feeling and spread to other members also. An un-satisfied employee usually becomes a source of spreading negative feelings among others which will ultimately affect work performance, the quality of service rendered.

7. **The requisite training for standard of excellence and performance (required by the employees)**

The responses in respect of the above question are tabulated in Chapter 5 and 6. We could see considerable and similar responses obtained from the two organisations under study.

Organisations	*Department of Industries & DICs*	*AmaraRaja Batteries*
New knowledge	63	30
Advanced skills	8	47
Confidence building	19	17
New knowledge & advanced skills	—	16

It may be pointed out here that the employees in Amara Raja Batteries are engaged in practical work in manufacturing the batteries. That is their main task and in the operational system they do interact with colleagues, subordinates and superiors. That is the social interaction often intensive in Amara Raja Batteries. On the other hand, the personnel in the Department of Industries are promotional agents are engaged in confidence building, motivating prospective entrepreneurs and guiding the ongoing entrepreneurs suggesting to them advanced and appropriate technology to upgrade their production, quality of products and their services.

The interaction of the personnel of the Department of Industries is mostly external with the client system. And in the case of Amara Raja Batteries it is mostly internal within the organisation.

8. Inter-personal relations

Inter-personal relations in any organisation are a crucial factor contributing to healthy and harmonious functioning of the employees from top to bottom. It is a critical human factor to which attention is to be paid. Vigilance over this is very necessary. Periodic study of incidents, complaints, disputes, reports or conflicts among the employees, which would indicate the harmonious or disharmonious climate in organisation. These observations and findings indicate that in respect of inter-personal relations could be studied in depth and appropriate training programmes are to be designed and conducted so that disharmony among the employees may be reduced or eliminated.

Inter personal relations with subordinates

In the present context, in respect to the two organisations understudy, in the case of Amara Raja Batteries surprisingly, 50 out of 110 respondents nearly (50%) did not respond, in respect to their relationship with their subordinates. In one sense, it may be interpreted that in respect to the relationship among the respondents with their subordinates may be unsatisfactory and as a kind of preference though they are unhappy with their subordinates behaviour and their support they remained silent and not to comment upon negatively and getting exposed. In another sense, the respondents are sensitive and prepared not to cause any ill feeling on the part of the subordinates and they remain silent in respect to this question. It may be pointed out here that in the case of Amara Raja Batteries, it is a closed society something like an extended family one could see the hesitancy on the part of super-ordinates commenting on the work behaviour of their subordinates.

In respect to Department of Industries, it is interesting to note that nearly the same number of people have indicated that they are happy (39) with the working and behaviour of their subordinates and on the other hand, 31 respondents have indicated that the work behaviour of the subordinates is very poor and they are very unhappy with their performance.

Inter-Personal Relations with colleagues

The nature of working relationships among the colleagues in Amara Raja Batteries seems to be good. About 72 respondents have indicated that they feel very happy in working with their colleagues. It means co- ordination of work among them vis-à-vis the work they carry out is smooth and fine. It is a positive indication of the smooth working of Amara Raja Batteries in general.

But when we come down to the Department of Industries we find a similar kind of happy working relationship among the colleagues expressed by the majority 66 out of 90. But it is note worthy in this case that 17 respondents out of 90 feel that the understanding and co-ordination of the work among the colleagues is not encouraging.

Inter- personal Relations with super-ordinates:

When we come to subordinates views on super-ordinates, it is really interesting and worth noting. In respect to Amara Raja Batteries, 48 respondents out of 110 did not respond which means that they are not satisfied with the work relationship with their super-ordinates. We should note here especially in the case of the subordinates even though they are unhappy in working with their superiors, they are hesitant as a common universal feature not to comment upon on their superiors for fear of likely negative consequences, ill treatment or punishment that they would suffer as the superiors would initiate such things. It is also interesting to mention here 19 respondents out of 110 responded that they are not at all satisfied in working with their superior officers. And at the same time, 5 feel very unhappy, 6 feel poor in working relationship with their superiors. This kind of a human relations in working is not uncommon. This kind of situation exists in most of the organisations as in the case of the present study.

When we come to the Department of Industries the following is the picture that is presented with work relationships with their super-ordinates.

47 respondents out of 90 feel happy and they have good relationships at the work situation with their superior personnel. A very small number (7) feel very happy in working with their super-ordinate personnel. It is also interesting to note here that 29 out of 90 respondents feel quite unhappy in working with their superior officers. There may be several reasons for this kind of situation-personal, prejudices, misunderstanding and incompetence on the part of the respondents.

9. Suggestions to improve work conditions by the employees

It may be noted here in the present study, the researcher had included a question seeking suggestions from the different categories of respondents, the ways to improve the organisations of these two sectors. The following are the suggestions offered by the Department of Industries and Amara Raja Batteries.

Based on the study of these two organisations the following suggestions emerge which may contribute to better relations among the staff, maximal utilization of the resources, realizing the goals and objectives of the respective organisations, creating employment and utilizing the natural resources available in an area and adopting the day to day advanced production technology and ultimately creating employment and in a larger sense bettering the living conditions of the employees and the management.

In the present study, the following suggestions emerge which may contribute to the effective, healthy and profit creating onward movement in both the organisations. It may be again mentioned here that Amara Raja Batteries is a profit oriented and commercial organisation where as the Department of Industries is a promotional and a welfare service agency. The suggestions made by the respondents of both the organisations are put together and are mentioned below:

1. Training should be given much importance so that employees' strengths and weaknesses are identified and also training is given in latest trends to meet the requirements of competition.
2. An informal climate is to be created to work enthusiastically.
3. Provide hygienic food to the employees who work in the night shifts as well as who work in the day shift.
4. Good inter-personal relations are created among the employees, reduce the duplication of work, co-operation among the employees is created, team work should be encouraged, shared vision is needed for the growth and development of any organization, openness and transparent atmosphere is created in respect of organizational improvement. To achieve all the above factors top management support is required.
5. The organizations should take up always innovative and challenging tasks. Decentralization and delegation of authority to the employees should be there.
6. Create pleasant environment to identify the

employees' abilities and improve the employee motivation.

Based on the researcher's personal interaction and observation vis-à-vis, the organisation and the respondents in respect to the kind of criteria for promotions, motivation or career advancement of the employees in summary the following suggestions or ideas emerged from the respondents. First, we will speak of Amara Raja Batteries, then we look into the Department of Industries in Andhra Pradesh.

Criteria for promotions and motivation of employees in Amara Raja Batteries:

1. Performance factor: Performance is a principal criterion for promotions in the organisation encompassing, clarity in communication, interpersonal relations, team coping up. Whenever there is a challenging task and increased demand with limited time specification or the employees are to gear up work intensively, extra hours, to meet the targets and providing leadership. Seniority and experience stand in second place for promotions in this organization.
2. Incentives:
   a. Special allowance based on performance: It may be mentioned here some money is provided to the employees when they exceed in their performance in meeting target fixed in their case. When the employees are rewarded in respect to a target, which he achieved that itself is a motivating factor. It is not something final. This kind of recognition and monetary encouragement to the employees plays as a motivator to the other employees in the organisation. It sets as a norm and example.
   b. Group Insurance (health): For the benefit of the employees group insurance scheme is available in

Amara Raja Batteries where as it is not existing in the Department of Industries.

c. Employee Benevolent Fund: It may be noted here that there is Benevolent Fund which goes to Amara Raja Battery employees in the event of death of an employee. Within 24 hours the children or the relatives of the person who passed away will be paid Rs.25,000/- so that bereaved family may cope up funeral expenses and gradually settle down to normal life.

d. Superannuation Scheme (Insurance): Further in the organisation this scheme is linked with Life Insurance Corporation. The regular premium will be paid by the company itself. In case of demise of the employee before he retires, the employee gets total gross money and it will be paid by the Insurance Company to the family. And also either spouse or one child from the family gets employed in the organisation.

Besides performance they also look into experience, the behaviour and educational qualifications.

- The strength of Amara Raja Batteries is the quality and the style of management. There are no trade unions among the employees.
- The continuance of the employee in his job depends on his performance. His continuance in the organisation depends on his performance and there is no security of job when an individual employee fails in his expected performance

Now we look at the Department of Industries:

Criteria for promotion: Promotion based on seniority of the employee. Instances have surfaced that a person who joins as an Industrial Promotion Officer retires in the same position. One could imagine interest, commitment, quality of performance among such employees that they will have no promotions throughout their service and retires as mentioned above with the same designation when he joined the organisation. Even though the employees who continue in the same job and technically qualified (B. Tech and M. Tech.) ones. One may attribute this kind of discouraging situation to the employee himself or to the system of the department.

Since it is a department run by Government, there are no other incentives except pension.

9

FINDINGS AND SUGGESTIONS

There is no universal standard in respect to Human Resource Development. At the outset, whatever may be the components or elements that stand for Human Resource Development, there are negligible qualifications of those elements or components except in respect to the requisite physical facilities, material benefits. One can think of two major aspects in Human Resource Development. One is organic and another is inorganic – behavioural and motivational side.

The primary concern in respect to Human Resource Development is on the part of the organisation. In their interest of growth and development they may have to plan to introduce and maintain Human Resource Development components both objective and subjective in their own interest. Incidentally efforts made by the organisation in counselling and providing training to the employees may be considered as secondary. Any benefit from Human Resource Development is fallout in respect to the employees. It does not mean that the organisation is not interested in the growth, development and welfare of its employees. As mentioned above the primary concern for them is their own interest. Sometimes we see the employees and the organisations have a lot of diversity. There is a mutual inter-dependency between the organisation and the employees. One side simply cannot ignore the other side. One principle in Human Resource Development is towards establishing and sustaining harmonious, productive, mutually beneficial, advancement of progress in respect to the organisation and its employees.

The Human Resource Development is an essential component in educating, enlightening, motivating and nurturing towards committed and better performance in the role assigned and assumed by the employee. We cannot think of a universal standard in respect to what degree the philosophy and the principles of Human Resource Development are understood, recognized in an attempt to make these principles inducted in an organisation. All over the world in different types of organisations the importance and contribution of Human Resource Development is recognized. But the way in which it is translated into action differs from the Departments of Government and Private Sector.

The present study is an attempt to examine to the extent to which the Human Resource Development and tenets are adhered to and put into action.

As we have pointed out in the previous chapters we find a significant difference in adopting the main elements of Human Resource Development factors in the case of Department of Industries, Government of Andhra Pradesh and a private organisation – Amara Raja Batteries. The following are the differences and similarities in between two organisations.

In respect of training: Though pre-entry training is similar to both organisations there is a significant difference in imparting the training. The Department of Industries, Government of Andhra Pradesh, conducts pre-entry training programmes for 21 days in a general sense. But on the other hand, in Amara Raja Batteries, though it is conducted for 3 – 5 days, it is more practice oriented related to the jobs or functions in the company. It is in the case of Amara Raja Batteries, a specific programme acquainting the nature of production activities and the standards they are adhered to and the way in which they are expected to perform their job in delivery of batteries to a wide variety of consumers.

In respect of behaviour and commitment of the employees we find largely common and similar practices in both the organisations, but when it comes to the sense of belonging we find that the employees of the Amara Raja Batteries show more concern and they express and demonstrate their feelings as if they are part of the organisation. Though they are not owners of the organisation, in a sense their work and concern for the organisation, show they are the partners of the organisation.

This sense of belonging we find in a large number of private production and service organisations, which of course is profit oriented and also which function in competition with national and international organisations engaged in similar kind of production and service activities.

We may point out here that there is a considerable extent and practice of delegation of authority and decentralization of decision making more in the case of Amara Raja Batteries than in the Department of Industries, Government of Andhra Pradesh. As usual it is a hierarchical system with several steps in between. The planning and decision making largely depends on the Ministry concerned followed by the chief of the Directorate of Industries. Occasionally they may seek information or guidelines for the direction from the top and middle level management. But largely the policy and decisions are made at the apex level. The implicit job on the part of the entire hierarchy in the department is to follow and implement the decision. It is something to take note of as a lesson. The employees at different levels in their action for promoting and guiding entrepreneurial activities among the prospective entrepreneurs and ongoing entrepreneurs have the first hand knowledge of the prospects and problems related to small scale industrial promotion in the State. It is really regrettable to note normally the top administration or the ministry concerned very often does not bother to study the real factors and problems related to small scale industrial promotion. The kind of administration carried out by the Department of Industries is a stereotype one.

When it comes to the participation in decision making and formulating the objectives, it may be pointed out here in both the organizations it is similar in nature. The involvement of the employees except top executives in decision making by management/higher authority is almost nil in both the organisations.

When it comes to Contribution of Training it is felt by the respondents of both the organisations that training is essential and there are similarities of impressions on the part of the respondents on both sides. But when it comes to the training programmes organised by the Department of Industries which are general in nature and stereotype ones, as contrary to job function, objective, expected performance on the part of the employees.

In respect to the proposed training programmes imparted to the employees it is felt important on the part of the respondents of both the organisations. One significant difference in respect to Amara Raja Batteries is that it is a commercial enterprise; the emphasis is laid in training, in advanced technology in the manufacture of batteries. All the time their eyes and concern are on how best they can stand competition in the market. Therefore all the time they are seeking and looking for better ways of knowledge and skill development on the part of its employees so that their products will have high demand in the market. On the other hand, there is no such challenge and compulsion on the part of the

Department of Industries. Principally it is a promotional agency not target oriented. Of course, the department objectives sow certain degree of achievement in promoting small scale enterprises.

Working environment

We find positive indications in the case of Amara Raja Batteries, but when we come to the Department of Industries 11 respondents out of 90 indicated that they are not satisfied with the working environment. This environment concept may relate to the work infrastructural facilities, colleagues, subordinates and super-ordinates. It is really note worthy here, though the number is small (11), expressing their dissatisfaction with the working condition from the Department of Industries needs soul searching. It needs a probe in detail as to what factors really make the working conditions not satisfactory. Whether it is physical, material, behavioural, human and managerial is to be looked into and studied so that we may eliminate this aspect of unsatisfactory feeling on the part of considerable number of employees in the Department of Industries.

Requisite training wanting by the employees: Usually in any organisation the management may in a routine way organise some training programmes. Sometimes based on Survey and Study and the level of performance excellence on the part of the employees, the management develops and organises need based training programmes. It is rather unusual and rare the participants themselves suggesting to the management certain areas or themes, training programmes to be organised and conducted. This initiative is both from Amara Raja Batteries and Department of Industries. It is a positive indicator on the part of the employees in recognizing themselves the knowledge and skill which is wanting in them and towards which they would like to acquire new knowledge and develop advanced skills for their own progress and at the same time contribute to the enrichment of the organisation, as listed out in Chapter 6, 7 & 8, the kind of training programmes suggested by the participants. This initiative and reflection on the part of the employees is quiet appreciable.

Inter-Personal Relations with subordinates, Colleagues and super-ordinates The kind of working relationships among the colleagues in both the organizations is smooth and cordial but in the relationship between subordinates and super-ordinates appear to be rather poor. In this context, we may mention the nature of work in Amara Raja Batteries is technical and manufacturing and often we find monitoring the work of subordinates by the superior officials who are technically well qualified. In Amara Raja Batteries there is work-related intimate face to face relation - friendly and antagonistic. When it comes to Department of Industries it is mostly promotional extensional work, the officials working in the different points in the district or state. In their case, there is minimal personal contact except through periodic meetings, written correspondence and reports. This is the major difference between Amara Raja Batteries & Department of Industries.

Suggestions offered for improving work conditions by the employees:

The employees in both the cases under study offered some suggestions for improving work conditions in the organisation. The suggestions are general in nature not specific. These suggestions are mentioned in Chapter 6 and 7.

There is one significant managerial conduct in Amara Raja Batteries, since it is a factory there is a prescribed uniform for all the employees while they are on work. The Managing Director of Amara Raja Batteries is Ramachandra Naidu Galla, also, while in the factory premises, wears the same uniform identical with all the employees. It is very rare and unusual for Management, Director or Chairman of Companies wear the uniform that is prescribed for the employees.

Here, it is in the case of Amara Raja Batteries, the principle of closeness and intimacy between the management and the work force he is made identical through uniform. It is a symbolic expression on the part of the Managing Director that he is one among the employees, though he is the Managing Director. This has a socio-physiological effect on the part of the employees.

Whenever the Managing Director, Amara Raja Batteries visits, the factory, he goes around all the sections/departments and he greets the employees. This way the Managing Director maintains personal contact with the workers. This simple courtesy on the part of the Managing Director enthuses the employees and ensures positive attitude towards the management and commitment on their part towards their work.

Suggestions Based on the Research Findings

Along with the administration of the structured questionnaires to a selected sample of respondents in both the organisations the researcher in the course of the study had an opportunity of observing in a general sense working of the system in both the organisations.

At this point of time there is no question of disagreement in respect to the promotive and facilitating role of Human Resource Development in organisations – whatever may be the type. Over decades right from the inception of industrial revolution organisations have gradually recognized and learnt, the significant and vital elements contributing to the organisational development simultaneously making the employees contented and committed to the task. Human Resource Development is an increasing, educational and motivating factor.

Based on the present study, the organisations in general Government and Private have to examine the present system of functioning and identify the present quantum of composition in the organisational structure and operation and identify the areas in which Human Resource Development as a facilitating and promoting factor is to be inducted into the system. It may be training the employees in relevant and needed areas, establishing day to day cordial relations with them and creating a sense of belongingness on the part of the employees to the organisation. This kind of approach and action may not be possible in a day or two or within a short time.

A tradition is to be established where the vital component of Human Resource Development constitutes a standard operational system. In such a tradition and practice one will find satisfaction of achievement on the part of the management and a sense of contribution to the organisation on the part of the employees. Once the significant contributing components are recognized in Human Resource Development the management may have to examine where they are vis-à-vis the Human Resource Development factor in their organisations. Human Resource Development as mentioned elsewhere several times is a Human Factor. You may ignore other factors and requisite conditions for grooming to make any system successful, but not the Human factor – the Human Resource Development. It may be pointed out here that we have not reached a terminal point in enriching the major factors that constitute the body of Human Resource Development. Each organisation may have to with all earnestness examine where they are, what they are, where they want to be, what they want to be in achieving the objectives and the goals of their organisation and at the same time identify and concretize the essential contributing factors of Human Resource Development for the success of their organisation.

At this point, we are not exaggerating or simply highlighting the indispensable and wholesome Human Resource Development component in organisations. It may be related to training, human relations, Inter-personal communication, work culture and working environment, the support and motivation provided to the employees and gradually generating a homely and harmonious atmosphere in the organisation whether it is on premises of the campus, office or in the field. Today, no one anywhere in the world can deny Human Resource Development as a invariable vital component for the success of any productive activity or service.

These ideas emerge based on the study of interestingly a private commercial organisation and Department of Industries, Government of Andhra Pradesh, which are entirely two different systems with different objectives. The former (Amara Raja Battery) is a commercial enterprise interested in selling and popularizing their products and making the profits. Whereas the Department of Industries, Government of Andhra Pradesh, is encouraging the people to develop, utilize the natural resources available, producing the products and services and thus creating self-employment and self-reliance.

It is something difficult for any organisation Private or Government to declare that it has reached finale or the peak in regard to the ideal Human Resource Development components, physical and behavioural aspects wholly infused in the working system. There may be a few organisations especially in the private sector who have realized early the importance of Human Resource Development in organisation as a vital and contributing factor. When it comes to the departments under Government, it is not a charge levelled against them. The Human Resource Development factor here is not as rich as we generally find in private organisations whether it is in India or elsewhere.

Based on this present study as indicated above every organisation Private or Government, small or large may have to bestow attention to Human Resource Development in its various forms or dimensions which would enrich and sustain the quantity of performance on the part of the employees simultaneously contributing to the objectives, goals and principles of the organisations Private or Government.

While we speak of Human Resource Development and its contribution to the progress of the organisation enthusing and motivating the employees towards their contribution to the growth and development of organisation, it has been observed that:

- Inter personal relations have a great impact on day to day dealings or interacting amongst colleagues. The situation should not let personality clashes interfere with the performance of the employees at work.
- Further it may be stated that it is quiet evident and well-known fact tested over time that any organisation interested in improving its services the profits, needs to devclop its employees' competencies for improved performance.
- It is also very important to be recognized and pay attention towards winning loyalty of employees in the organisation. But once it is achieved, employees contribution and involvement help the organisations at the bottomline.
- In order to promote and translate into action the vital Human Resource Development components, an attempt is to be made through training, reducing or eliminating the skill gap related to the operational requirements.
- Further in order to compete in the global economy there is a need to critically examine the employees' competence and identifying the deficiencies in them and based on these deficiencies one may have to go in for structuring and organizing relevant training

programmes followed by individual counselling in order to reduce deficiencies among the employees.

- It is believed that all organisations in the world especially private in order to long last in operational service have to bestow attention and create opportunities for life long learning on the part of the employees.
- Human Resource Development is not one time act. It is a continuous carefully sustained and integrated input in every kind of organisation, whether it is commercial or service oriented.

It may be pointed out here that once the managements understand the importance of HRD in the organisations then they have to go for a planned change. This planned change may be in respect of training of the employees based on the needs, organisational development, career development of the individuals etc. When the top management goes for a planned change it leads to individual development which in turn helps in organisational development.

If the above model is followed it will contribute a lot in implementing HRD aspects in any organisation. In the present study, the sample units are Government and private sectors. In Government sector as we have observed there is no thrust on need based training, career development of the individuals which is a hindrance to the organisational development. This is responsible for poor productivity, less quality, no innovativeness among the employees. Though there is a thrust on need based training in the Amara Raja Batteries the private sector sample unit proper planning with regard to career development and inter personal relations of individuals needs to be strengthened. If the HRD model developed by P.A. McLagan is adopted by any organisation it will contribute a lot to Human Resource Development.

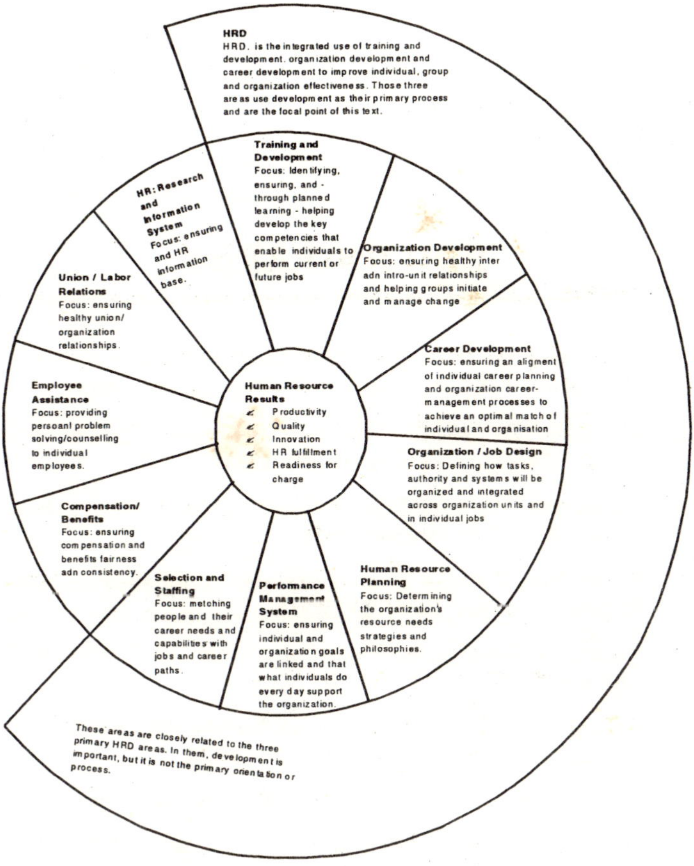

HRD MODEL

Source: From P.A. McLagan (1989). Models for HRD PRACTICE, Training and Development Journal, 41:53.

BIBLIOGRAPHY

1. Agarwal, R.D., *Dynamics of Personnel Management in India*, New Dilhi, Tata McGraw-Hill Publishing Co., 1977.
2. An article "Be Specific about your aim, know what you want," *Deccan Chronicle* on August 30th 2003.
3. An article "Get on Top of Conflict Situations," *Deccan Chronicle* on 11th October 2003.
4. An article "Manage Your Manpower" published in Deccan Chronicle on November 29th 2003.
5. An article "Staying in Power for a long Time" published in The Times of India on July 6th 2005.
6. An article "Win The Loyalty of Employees" published in Deccan Chronicle on November 22nd 2003.
7. Aswarthappa "*Human Resource Management*" 2004
8. Basu, K.S., *New Dimensions in Personnel Management*. Macmillan & Co., New Delhi, 1979.
9. Beer et al, *Human Resource Management : A General Managers Perspective*, New York, The Free Press
10. Boxall, P; Strategic Human Resource Management: Beginnings of a New theoritical sophistication, Human Resource Journal, 2(3), 1992.
11. C.S. Venkataratnam and B.K. Srivastava, *Personnel Management and Human Resources*, Tata McGraw-Hill, New Delhi, 1991.
12. Cynthia D.Fisher, et al., *Human Resource Management*, Houghton Miffin, 1997.

13. David A. Decenzo & Stephen P. Robbins, *Personnel / Human Resource Management,* Prentice Hall of India Private Ltd., New Delhi, 1996.

14. Donals F. Harvey, *Strategic Management and Business Policy,* 2nd Ed., Columbus, Merrill Publishing, 1988.

15. Dr. Aryasri, *Management Science,* 2004

16. Edwin B. Flippo, *Personnel Management,* fourth edition, McGraw-Hill, New York, 1984,

17. Fombrum, Tichy, N.M and Devanna, M.A, '*Strategic Human Resource Management*', New York, Wiley, 1984.

18. George T. Milkovich & Johri W. Boudreau, '*Human Resource Management,* Chicago, Irwin, 1997.

19. George T.Milkovich and Johri W. Boudreau, *Human Resource Management,* Chicago, Irwin, 1997.

20. Gratton,*et al,* '*Strategic HRM : Corporate Rhetoric and Human Reality*', Oxford University Press.

21. http//www.rci.rutgers.edu/-sjacksox/PDF/ understanding HRManagement in the organizational context.

22. Ian Beardwell and Len Holden, *Human Resource Management,* London Macmillan, 1995.

23. Ian Beardwell and Len Holden, *Human Resources Management,* Macmillan Ltd., 1996.

24. Ian Beardwell and Len Holden, Op. Cit..

25. M.M. Bagali, 'Employee Empowerment: Renaissance Strategies for creating high performance organisation', Paper presented at the XXXII National Convention of Indian Society for Training and Development, January 17-19, 2002, Hyderabad, , Managing the ever changing organisation.

26. Nabaghana Pany & Ashok Kumar Rath, 'Emerging role of HRM in Changing Business Scenario', Paper presented at the XXXII National Convention of Indian Society for Training and Development, January 17-19, 2002, Hyderabad, Managing the ever changing organisation..

27. Pareek: U. and T. V. Rao, '*Designing and Managing HR Systems*', Oxford & IBH Publishing Company, New Delhi, 1981.

28. Peters and Waterman, 'Describing the Best Companies in search of excellence of H.R. Strategy, 1982.

29. Prof. T.V. Rao, HRD Audit, A Division of Saga Publications, 1999.

30. Professor Janis Langstaff, Reading material on Human Resource Management prepared by MIM.

31. Rao T.V. & D.F. Pereira, '*Recent experiences in Human Resources Development*, Oxford & IBH Publishing Company, New Delhi, 1981.

32. Sikula Andrew F. & John F. McKenna, *The Management of Human Resources*, John Wiley, New York, 1984.

33. Storey, 'Management of Human Resources ' Oxford, Blackwell, 1989.

34. Storey, Op. Cit..

35. Training Reading material on "Human Resource Management" given by Dr. MCR HRD IAP.

36. Training Reading material on "Planning & Management of Human Resource in Government" Given by Dr. MCR HRD IAP.

37. Training Reading material on "Strategic Human Resource Management" supplied by ASCI K.

38. Walton, 'From control to commitment in the work place' Harvard Business Review, March-April 1985.

39. Wayne F. Cascio, *Managing Human Resources*, McGraw-Hill, 1995.

40. William B. Werther, Jr and Keith Davis, *Human Resources and Personnel Management*, fourth Edition McGraw-Hill, New York, 1993.

41. William B. Werther, Jr. & Keith Davis, '*Human Resources and Personnel Management*, McGraw Hill, 1994.

42. William P. Anthony, et al., Strategic Human Resource Management, Dryden Press, 1993,.

INDEX

■■■